THE LISTENER

BOOKS BY ALLEN WHEELIS

The Way Things Are

The Life and Death of My Mother

The Doctor of Desire

The Scheme of Things

On Not Knowing How to Live

How People Change

The Moralist

The End of the Modern Age

The Desert

The Illusionless Man

The Seeker

The Quest for Identity

ALLEN WHEELIS

THE LISTENER

A PSYCHOANALYST EXAMINES HIS LIFE

W. W. NORTON & COMPANY
NEW YORK • LONDON

For information about permission to reproduce selections from
this book, write to Permissions, W. W. Norton & Company,
500 Fifth Avenue, New York, NY 10110.

The text of this book is set in FF Scala
with the display set in Weiss
Desktop composition by Gina Webster
Manufacturing by Haddon Craftsmen, Inc.
Book design by Lane Kimball Trubey

Library of Congress Cataloging-in-Publication Data

Wheelis, Allen, 1915–
The listener : a psychoanalyst examines his life / Allen Wheelis.
p.   cm.
ISBN 13: 978-0-393-33637-5
1. Wheelis, Allen, 1915–   . 2. Psychoanalysts—United
States—Biography. I. Title.
BF109.W44A3   1999
150.19'5'092—dc21   99-21607
[B]   CIP

W. W. Norton & Company, Inc.
500 Fifth Avenue, New York, N.Y. 10110
www.wwnorton.com

W. W. Norton & Company Ltd.
10 Coptic Street, London WC1A 1PU

1 2 3 4 5 6 7 8 9 0

for ILSE

CONTENTS

Foreword 9

I The Unruly Trio 13

II The Hidden Piano 19

III Good-bye, Mama 75

IV The Stranger 99

V Psychoanalysis 119

VI Girls 127

VII Wife 139

VIII The Architect 173

IX The Little Boy 179

X Voices from the Couch 193

XI The Flying Dutchman 207

XII *Rackety-Rackety-Rackety* 229

FOREWORD

PIECES OF MYSELF are scattered like shards throughout my work. Here they are brought together, others added, made into a mosaic. Not yet a self-portrait, more a self-sketch, this is what I see in the darkening mirror.

It *is* glory—to have been tested, to have had our little quality and cast our little spell. . . . A second chance—*that's* the delusion. There never was to be but one. We work in the dark—we do what we can—we give what we have. Our doubt is our passion and our passion is our task. The rest is the madness of art.

—Henry James

I

THE UNRULY TRIO

WHEN I PICK up a novel, I look first for the sexual passages. I want to know what this author thinks can happen between a man and a woman. I discover the girl undressing, examine her undergarments, see her twisting and moaning under her lover—all this without yet knowing her name, nothing of her interests, values, family, education, job, or friends. I go right to the limit, the far edge. Before learning whether it's safe for her even to have coffee with this guy or to go for a walk, I have her skirt up, her legs spread wide.

It never happens this way in real life. Unfortunately. The cup of coffee and the walk on the beach are mandatory. We can't skip these first steps; we're too frightened. Read properly, one page after another, the novel, if it's good, will portray a relationship as it develops in real life; read in my greedy and desperate way, it shows a feverishly speeded-up affair, a break-neck development, an unreal intimacy.

How interesting it would be—how wonderful!—to have in real life an affair so purged of props, of exposition, so telescoped. Would save a lot of time. Be far more exciting. And more dangerous. Who knows? I might find myself between the legs of a murderess, a vampire's mouth on my throat.

When I pick up a novel and seek out the sexual passages, it happens at times that these turn out to be pornography. Suddenly I am seized, locked in, like metal to magnet: nothing could tear this book from my hands. But even while devouring it in this rapt way, I know that something evil is being offered to me, and that it is something evil in me that is responding. And I know, further, that this lunge into the forbidden is limited, that it will end soon, and that I will then put this book from me, will reject with aversion what I have but a moment ago so avidly consumed.

ACTUALLY IT'S NOT quite true that I look *first* for the sexual passages; that's what I go for by default, not finding that for which I really hunger—which is subtle and elusive, lacks the hypnotic lure of evil, and is far more rare. All voices claim to grasp reality, but I don't believe them. They sound synthetic, like those computer-made voices in electronic mail. The reality they present is window- display, not what happens in the street. I seek the sound of a human voice. A voice that bears witness, attests the way things really are. This means a voice that has freed itself, usually with great suffering and effort, of the vast corruption of language and experience, of the clichés, the jargon, and the kitsch, of that sea of deceit and pretense in which we drift. When I hear it, I feel respect, I turn back to page one and read carefully. Such voices are rare, are usually drowned out by the din around us.

A HUMAN VOICE is one that bears the awareness of death—
that once-only-once-and-never-again resonance. Sex and
death, eternal antagonists, forever contending, forever overturning and contradicting each other. And beyond these difficult two, that impossible third, love, inextricably commin-
gled.   *Sex, death, love*
   This is the text of my life, this unruly trio.

THE ADVERTISEMENT FOR the travel agency shows a black-
haired girl in the surf at Acapulco: black bikini, shoulders
hunched forward exposing the heft of breasts. She is laughing
hysterically, her long hair hanging wet, one hand raised to the
side of her face in a gesture of vulnerability, a movement that
bespeaks (so I imagine) a capacity for passion and for tender-
ness. I study the picture with an intentness both savage and
desolate. Desire springs up, envelops her, pushes beyond the
presenting laughter, beyond the innocent beach games, into
the hotel behind her, takes her into the privacy of a luxurious
room where an incandescent eroticism, the heart and soul of
this vacation, is to occur. Is this the way the adman wants me
to think? It works! It works!
   In the hospital, a nurse walks toward me down a long hallway: tight white uniform pulled into slight transverse wrinkles
across the full hips (I slow my pace), white stockings, full
round face, Italian romantic style, broad soft mouth, very dark
eyes and eyebrows (I stop), white skin, glistening black hair,
straight and soft, drawn back loosely across her ears (I'm back-
ing up a bit now). Just before she passes, the liquid eyes look
up, and for a moment the face is transformed with a smile of
breath-catching trustfulness.
   Longing mounts, becomes frantic. If I had one, I'd want the
other. I want both, I want them all. I ascribe to these creatures
a quality of heaven, a gift of redemption, a love that would
enable me to become what I am not, will never be.

GREAT BEAUTY INFLICTS a wound. Private and somehow shameful. It can neither be acknowledged nor complained about. A deep, burning pain. It will not go away. The pain is the longing; the wound is the knowing that the longing can never be fulfilled, that, like hell, it will go on forever, always there, always inside. It can be pushed aside by exigencies of work or by the press of dailiness, but never extinguished. Beauty calls it forth as from a dark cavern, from some forlorn hidden place in me, and I know then that this longing is my essence, that this private unacknowledged thing is what I am, the one true photograph of myself. I keep it hidden, in a secret compartment, in that submerged cavern. Once or twice in a lifetime, if I'm lucky, I might venture to show it to someone I love.

And what might that photograph reveal? Do I allow even myself to see? A vast beach perhaps, stretching out in the distance endlessly, and one solitary figure, a woman. She looks out over an empty sea. She is waiting without hope. She knows no one will come. She waits for me, and I seek her always. We will never meet.

What is the objective, the public reality? Of that, there are many photographs. Many people could come up with them. They would show a lot, many different things. You would see me with my family, in my study, on the Golden Gate Bridge leaning over the rail, working with patients, playing tennis, having lunch with my publisher, conversing with friends—all true, all real, all surface. That's all that can be known of me, and, knowing it, you would miss me entire. I will have fallen through your net. The reality of my being is that hidden photograph.

This is the kind of reality I seek in fiction. I'm not interested in the everyday reality of a man's job, family, fishing trips, clothes, business deals, the house he lives in or how it's furnished, or whether he becomes a senior partner in the law firm. Unless, magically, such details become signs pointing to a hidden reality, I am impatient, skip forward. I grant them some slight relevance in establishing a context, a place, but what I'm after is the hidden reality. The man's longing. How does he experience it? What does he do with it?

Specifically, I want to know what this author believes can happen between a man and a woman. I believe that we, all of us, are locked within the prison of self, that in this prison we yearn for release by fusion with another. And I have come to believe that this fusion, this transcendent love and oneness, is an illusion, that it can be achieved if at all only briefly, that as a vision of a possible state of being it is fool's gold, that the reality is that we have to live in the solitary confinement of our tiny cell, and that, should we briefly escape this cell, we will soon be back in it.

It is the ubiquity of conflict that dooms the fusion. For conflict forces the lovers back into their corners. One cannot avoid that estrangement by finding the lover with whom one has a perfect fit; for *she* does not exist. And one cannot avoid it by finding a meek lover who will renounce conflict, will always give in—the Japanese wife solution! For, as she sacrifices her separate and contending interests to maintain the fusion, she accrues a resentment that, however rigorously silenced, will itself destroy the fusion.

But no matter. The yearning won't go away. It is ubiquitous and forever, and when I pick up a novel, I'm wanting to see what this author has found out about it. Perhaps he denies it altogether, is unaware even of its existence. Then I'm not interested; I lay the book aside. Or perhaps the longing is portrayed as fulfillable: The pain is a mistake, not necessary but neurotic; it can be overcome with resignation or with religion or wisdom or psychoanalysis; the good life is possible, requires only that one come to terms, make a good adjustment. Then the author is a liar or a fool, and his work is escapism, not art.

For art—however fragmented, bizarre, surrealistic its means—is always a quest for the real, it seeks to grasp the way things are. And when an author persuades me that he is honestly and ruthlessly in pursuit of the real, then I am intensely interested in what he has found out about love.

I seek out the sexual passages because it is here, in these restless, intimate touchings, that the hidden longing is most likely to surface, here that I may see its face. And here that it may be fulfilled. But rarely! rarely! and only for a moment—while what we want is deep, deep eternity.

The cruelty, violation, and sadism that lurk within sexuality are born of that transience. To come so close, to have it for a moment, and then, unavoidably, to lose it, to see it slip away—this evokes rage, a powerful surge of destructiveness. One wants to devour her, to soil her, to destroy her—all because one can't stand to lose what one has come so close to having, which is the only thing in life *worth* having, and which one did, for a moment, actually have.

WHAT IS THIS, anyway? one of my patients asks from the couch. *Do you guys have an explanation? Is this an infantile conflict—to be analyzed? Or the way things are—to be accepted?* Looking back over my now long life, what should one say of the pain and the longing? This is the human condition? Or, He was not well analyzed?

And if the latter, what possibly can *well analyzed* mean?

II

THE HIDDEN PIANO

In the picture I sit on my father's knee. I am one year old. Can one say "I" of an infant eighty-one years away? On the other knee my sister, June, five years old. She restrains my foot, so I must have been kicking. Behind us my mother, a tall, slender woman, round face, smooth white skin, heavy dark luxuriant hair coiled loosely at the back of her head in a bun. She wears a white blouse with lace collar. Her folded hands rest on her husband's shoulder. She stands before the empty fireplace, the cold hearth, looks down on her young family. Her expression is enigmatic: proud, shy, perhaps smug. On the mantel a clock, hands frozen for all these years at eight minutes past eleven; it rests on a doily with scalloped border, embroidered flowers, and a message: *Daisies Won't Tell.* Behind the clock a mirror. My father wears a striped shirt with high white starched collar, dark tie. His Sunday best. He is thirty-two. It is 1916.

My father holds before me his gold watch. I am transfixed with desire, eyes wide and gleaming, face aglow.

Yes, I can say "I" of that infant; I recognize myself in that longing. It's mine still, only now without an object. Then, a watch would do, or a bird, or a leaf. The longing now is nameless, voiceless, a burning inward sun.

In the picture, my mother, my father, my sister all look at the watch. They are following my rapturous gaze, sharing my experience of a longing that still knows what it wants, something tangible, something right there, within reach. For their separate and mute longings have already submerged, become nameless, as soon will mine. I show them a lost paradise. Try as they will, they will never find it. Nor will I.

IN 1898, EIGHTEEN years before this picture, my father, Morris Wheelis, then sixteen years old, left his father's farm and came to Marion, Louisiana, to go to school. He walked the eight miles, carrying his belongings on his back, and went to Mr. Dean's store, where he was to live. He went to high school in the red-brick school, worked in the store, had his meals in Mr. Dean's house, and slept on a cot in the back of the store where the grain was kept.

He was tall, had a bony, angular face, and a manner of reserve and composure. Upon being addressed, he would look steadily into the eyes of the speaker, listening with such still intentness as to suggest disbelief. And when the speaker had finished, Morris would not reply immediately, but would continue in silence to gaze into the other's eyes, as if listening now to what had *not* been said. During those few moments he would seem to bring what he had just heard into relation with everything else he knew that had a bearing, and only then would he reply. What he said in this deliberate way had an air

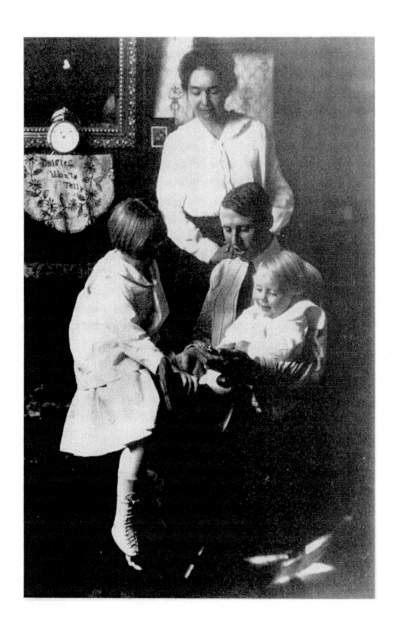

of finality, and was rarely modified or retracted. He worked hard and became well liked by Mr. Dean and by the people who entered the store to buy or who sat on the porch to talk. When he had time off, he went hunting, became known as a marksman, someone who could drop a running squirrel from the top of a sweet gum tree with one shot from a long barrel .22 rifle.

Marion was then a town of about two hundred people situated in a forest of virgin pine in the northern part of Louisiana. The nearest towns of greater size were Ruston and Monroe, each about forty miles away—a long day's journey by horse and buggy over winding, red clay roads, dusty in dry weather and treacherously slick in wet. Approaching Marion from Monroe, one's first view of the town would be from the crest of a low hill.

Off to the right was Aunt Alice's place, an ancient house which was said to have been used as a storehouse for food by the Confederate Army. A little further, in a grove of trees, were the Methodist and Baptist churches, each painted white with a small belfry and steeple, and no more than a hundred yards apart. Beyond the churches was the new red-brick schoolhouse, which had four rooms. Passing over a creek and mounting a low incline, one came then to the center of town—two red stores, each a long, narrow building extending back fifty yards from the street. One bore the sign: O.H. THOMPSON, MERCHANT AND COTTON BUYER; the other: J.H. DEAN, GENERAL MERCHANDISE. The space between these stores formed the village square, where horses were tethered and wagons loaded. The square was completed by a livery stable on one side and by Dr. Thompson's residence on the other. On any summer afternoon one could see three or four men lounging on the benches in front of the stores. They wore straw hats tilted back on their heads, and their shirt-sleeves were hitched up with colored garters. They looked on strangers in silence with a casual but curious stare.

At a distance of ten miles, through dense forests, ran the Ouachita River, the principal avenue of contact with the outside world. Its waters rose in late winter and spring, became muddy and turbulent, and sometimes flooded the lowlands. But in summer and fall it was a clear stream, seventy-five yards wide, running a winding course between banks of luxuriant vegetation. Bayous opened their still mouths to the river's edge. They bore such names as *De l'Outre* and *De Siard*. In a small boat, one could enter these stagnant channels and reach swamps of unearthly stillness. Hidden limbs of submerged trees reached up and touched the bottom of the boat like huge dead fingers. Banks were vague and insubstantial, and over them an alligator might occasionally be seen to slither. The overhanging branches of tremendous, devitalized trees, parasitized beyond recognition by the sorrowful Spanish moss, formed twilight caverns. It was the home of copperheads and cottonmouth water moccasins and of the heron whose sudden scream would shatter the silence. After an initial flapping of wings, the angular white ghost would glide low over the dead water, banking easily to avoid obstacles, wheeling and turning, rising and falling, skimming along over the still surface with only inches to spare, the white wings flickering through rotten branches, growing faint and inconstant, and disappearing finally in the gray silence.

OLIVER HAZARD THOMPSON, as a young country doctor in Alabama, had developed tuberculosis, and had been given three bits of advice by his father: to go west, to drink plenty of whiskey, and to stay out in the open air. He did all three. He left Alabama on horseback, rode into northern Louisiana, and settled in Union Parish. He built a store and an office in a clearing of trees on the red clay soil; a few years later he built a Methodist church for the circuit rider, and over the years the village of Marion formed itself around him. For many years he was the only doctor within a day's journey. He delivered babies, pulled teeth, sutured wounds, set broken bones. For many years he made his calls on horseback, but as he got older and the roads were better, he rode in a buggy. He wore high-top black shoes and a shiny black suit. A gold watch chain was always threaded across his vest. He had a full black beard that gradually turned gray. He always addressed his wife, Molly, as "Mrs. Thompson" ("Pass the biscuits, Mrs. Thompson"), and my mother, his firstborn, as "Daughter." He built his big house about a hundred yards from the store, and when dinner, as the noon meal was called, was ready, Molly would stand on the porch and ring the bell, and everyone in town would know that the doctor was closing the store and going home for dinner. He had nine children, of whom three died in infancy. Four boys and two girls survived. The oldest boy, Kleber, came back to Marion after college and took over the store. The youngest son, Clayton, never left home.

MORRIS WHEELIS FELL in love with Olive Thompson when she was thirteen, a black-haired girl with a face as soft and gentle as his was hard and angular. He decided then that eventually he would marry her, though it was not till some years later he told her of his decision. When he finished school, his wages were increased to ten dollars a month, in addition to food and lodging; and he saved this in preparation for his marriage. He did not like clerking in a store, and he did not like working for a boss. It was his intention to buy land and build a house and farm the land. When he was able to do this, he would be able to get married.

In 1904, Dr. James, just out of medical school, came to Marion to work with Dr. Thompson. Olive's head was turned, and that summer she had little time for Morris. Dr. James lived in the Thompson home and had his meals with the family. In the evening he sat with Olive in the porch swing, and on

Sunday afternoons took her for buggy rides. Morris made no protest and displayed no curiosity, but he watched them carefully. He knew when they finished dinner; for he could hear the creak of the porch swing from Mr. Dean's store. Lying on his cot in the back of the store among the sacks of corn, he could hear their laughter on the quiet summer nights. On Sundays he would watch them drive out of town in Dr. Thompson's buggy; when they had returned, he would walk along the way they had gone and would learn where they had been and where they stopped and how long they stopped.

When Dr. James sat down on the storefront to pass the time of day with Mr. Dean, Morris would observe him closely. His hands were white and uncallused; he always wore a coat and tie and hat; and his clothes were of a kind that could not be bought in Marion. Morris noticed, also, how he talked and what he talked about, and learned something of life in a city from what Dr. James said of Nashville, its trains and trolley cars and big buildings and telephones. He listened also to what other people said about his rival. Dr. James had an easygoing manner and a ready flow of conversation. He seemed to be a good physician, and people liked him.

In September, Dr. James left Marion and returned to New Orleans, where he had family connections. Olive was despondent for a while, but recovered, and Morris might then have bought his land and got married, but by then he had made a different decision. "If it's a doctor you like," he said to Olive, "it's a doctor I'll be." She protested against waiting four years, but he borrowed money from his brother, packed up his belongings, and set out for Nashville. He was graduated from medical school in 1908, returned to Marion, and began the life of a country doctor. He married Olive and built a small house, and in the course of time they had three children: a girl, June; a boy who died of infantile diarrhea; and me. They were deep in debt and they were very poor.

THE TOWN WAS changing. In 1903, sawmills had invaded the parish, and the great pine trees began to fall. A railroad was built to carry the logs, and the town blossomed. An apothecary set up shop, a post office was established, and mail was delivered every day. By 1915, there were thirty telephones and six automobiles, and the blacksmith sold gasoline and oil. The price of cotton fluctuated according to wars and the threat of wars. Planted with the same crop year after year, the land lost much of its fertility, which had not been great to start with. By 1917, the sawmills had cleared the parish and moved on, leaving fields of stumps in their wake. But they held the land they had acquired, and the town ceased to grow.

IN THE PICTURE, my mother is twenty-seven years old. In her climb up out of nothingness, this was perhaps the high point, the crest of consciousness, power, specialness. A year later the war swept up her husband, and she followed him with her two children to army camps in Alabama and Mississippi, then to Chattanooga, Tennessee, where she nursed him through a near-fatal influenza during the epidemic of 1918. In 1919, out of the army and a free man again, he returned to Marion, and took up again the practice of country medicine. Now they were out of the woods, they thought, now things would get easier. But within months he had tuberculosis. He lay flat in bed, and as the months passed, got worse. He should move to a drier climate, he was told; so he journeyed alone to San Antonio, where the dry, sunny climate would perhaps facilitate recovery, and for four months lay in a veterans' hospital.

Nothing was done for him, for there was no treatment except rest. Rest, however, was impossible; something like fury was burning inside him. He was still in debt to his brother, he was impatient to work, felt his career was just beginning, was straining to get on with it. He could not feel at home in this strange land of black dirt and level ground. The mesquite that people called "trees" would have been called scrub brush in Marion. If he had to rest, he would at least rest with his family. So he sent for Olive to come and bring the children.

With what was left of his savings he bought, for six hundred dollars, a house on the outskirts of San Antonio—a run-down house in a field of weeds and sunflowers. He had one porch of the house closed in with wire screens and glass, and this became his sickroom. He forced himself to lie in bed, but could not force himself to rest. He had his bed propped up so that he could see out, and was forever probing the countryside with binoculars. He watched the spiders and fed them flies; he had me put up an oatmeal box in a tree for the wrens; and when the sparrows would try to usurp this nest, Morris would shoot them from his sickbed with his .22 rifle, sometimes shooting through the screen wire. Here he lay and coughed, day after day, year after year, trying to get well.

"PRESS THE BUTT firmly against your shoulder. Now lower your cheek to the stock. Now look down the length of the barrel."

I am flooded with excitement, pride, delight. Longed for, yearned for, the wonderful weapon is now in my hands.

"The line of sight runs from the center of the target back to the topmost tip of the front sight, back along the barrel to the very bottom of the V of the rear sight. You understand?"

"Yes, sir."

"Only when these three things are lined up are you ready to fire. You understand?"

"Yes, sir."

"Never *pull* the trigger. *Squeeze* the trigger with a smooth and steady pressure, so smooth that the tripping of the hammer will not disturb the sighting of the rifle. You understand?"

"Yes, sir."

"Now go outside and take up your position under the awning of this porch. I'll tell you when and what to shoot."

Trembling with happiness, I do as he directs. He speaks to me now from his sickbed through the open window above my head. "You see the sparrow on the edge of the barn roof, about three feet from the wren's nest?"

"Yes, sir."

"Bring him into your sights."

I do so. "Yes, sir."

"Fire when you are ready."

I fire and the sparrow flies away. After a few minutes, I am given another target. Again I miss. "Hold the rifle absolutely still," comes the voice from above. Again I miss. "Come in the house!"

I stand beside his bed. He fixes me with a reproving stare, holds out his hand. With a wrenching sense of loss and unworthiness, I surrender the rifle. "I did what you said," I plead. I am desperate to have the gun back, to get another chance.

"Do you mean the rifle is defective?" His voice is full of scorn. "Does it have perhaps a crooked barrel?" He glares at me in bitter disappointment. "You did *not* do as I said. You did *not* line up the sights." He makes a gesture of annoyance and dismissal. "Go see if you can help your mother. Maybe you can do something useful in the house."

NO MEAL COULD begin without a blessing, and when I was seven years old this duty was delegated to me. When my father had been served his meal on a tray, the family would sit down to eat. We ate in the kitchen, and the table was so located that the chair in which I sat was visible from the porch. Occasionally, my father would lean out of bed, turn his head, and look at me. He did this less frequently as he grew weaker, but I never knew when I was being watched. When all of us were seated, we would bow our heads and I would say grace. I was not permitted to slur it or say it rapidly as a formality, but was obliged to speak reverently, in a loud, clear voice, so that my father, as well as God, could hear. "Lord, bless this food that now we take, and make us good for Jesus' sake. Amen." And sometimes from the porch would come a fatherly echo, "Amen." Then we would raise our heads and begin to eat.

Sometimes, however, the end of the blessing would be followed by a stinging reprimand. "Sit yourself up straight at that table, sir!" After a moment of bewilderment and fright, I would realize that I had been slouching in my chair, and would stiffen straightly and wait in silence. "Now you say that blessing again, sir!" I would thus be forced to repeat, and then would falteringly begin to eat, wondering if my father were still watching but afraid to look to find out.

Fear on edge [handwritten marginal note]

Every night about nine o'clock the family would gather to "talk with God." At this time the work of the day would be done, the dishes washed, the clothes ironed, the floor swept, and the sewing finished. For my mother, it was the most peaceful time of the day. June and I would be tired and perhaps sleepy. At this time, in summer, the night would have just arrived, and far away we might hear a train whistle or a dog bark. In winter, a wood-burning stove would warm the bedroom and porch while the rest of the house would be closed off and cold. Around the corners of the old house would be heard the thrilling, intimate shriek of a norther that had swept down through the flatlands of the great square states, whined through countless barbed-wire fences, across the Panhandle, and so to us. An unshaded bulb, hanging from a yellow, fly-specked cord, would light the room with a soporific glare. Because the underpinning of the house was high and screened only with latticework, the wind would pass not only above and around the house but also under it, lifting the floorboards and making them quiver, and invading the room through the cracks. Sometimes it would get in behind the rain-stained wallpaper, causing it to rattle and flap, and sometimes the house shook so that the room seemed to have lost contact with the ground, and we would have the sensation of being carried away by the wind.

These were the nights when strange noises were heard in the parts of the house that were closed off and dark. A door would open and close, the sound of footsteps would come from the adjoining room, an intruder would stumble against a chair in the kitchen. Tentacles of fear would grab at me, and my mother would start with alarm. Then we would look at Daddy, see that he was unperturbed, and would know that it was only the tricks of the wind playing with the decrepitude of the timeworn house.

At this time, about nine o'clock in the evening, winter and summer, the family convened for prayer.

Mama would sit in her chair on the porch, fold her hands, and wait. June and I would draw up chairs before the screen door. Then Daddy would take up the Bible and begin to turn through the pages. For perhaps five minutes we would sit in silence. This was a time for meditation. Speech and laughter were forbidden.

At this time each evening a familiar feeling of uneasiness would come over me. Though family prayer was a daily occurrence, I never did experience the contentment that is supposed to result from communion with God. Rather, when I saw Daddy open the gilt-edged book and felt the hush and solemnity of worship, I was beset by a sense of insincerity and unworthiness.

After looking meditatively through the Bible for a while in silence, Daddy would begin to read aloud—perhaps something from Proverbs.

"My son, forget not my law; but let thine heart keep my commandments; for length of days, and long life, and peace, shall they add to thee. Let not mercy and truth forsake thee: bind them about thy neck; write them upon the table of thine heart; so shalt thou find favor and good understanding in the sight of God and man. Trust in the Lord with all thine heart; and lean not unto thine own understanding. In all thy ways acknowledge him, and he shall direct thy paths. Be not wise in thine own eyes: fear the Lord and depart from evil. It shall be health to thy navel, and marrow to thy bones. Honor the Lord with thy substance, and with the first fruits of all thine increase; so shall thy barns be filled with plenty, and thy presses shall burst out with new wine. My son, despise not the chastening of the Lord; neither be weary of his correction. For whom the Lord loveth he correcteth; even as a father the son in whom he delighteth."

Slowly he would close the book and look up at his family. "Let us pray."

All of us, excepting Daddy, would get down on our knees and bow our heads, resting our arms on the chairs on which we had been sitting. We prayed in a customary order. After kneeling for a few moments in silence, Mama would begin. She prayed in the same soft voice in which she usually spoke, to which was added on these occasions only a note of humility. She could not mask her feeling, and from the way she spoke I would know how she felt. Usually she was calm and self-contained, but occasionally strain and worry would make themselves known by a pleading quality of voice. Rarely, she cried. When this happened I would feel a racking shame, and my own eyes would be wet.

"Dear heavenly Father, let the light of Thy blessing shine upon this family tonight. Help us to see Thy way, dear Lord. Make us to know the wisdom of Thy judgments. Not our will, but Thine, be done.

"But, O Lord, if it be Thy will, most humbly do we beseech Thee to restore health to this family. Bring back my husband's strength, dear Lord, that he may carry on Thy fight with renewed vigor, and praise Thy name all the days of his life.

"Bless these our children. May they never stray from the path of righteousness, but follow always in the footsteps of Jesus and strive to do Thy will.

"Forgive us our sins, dear Lord, and have mercy on our shortcomings; for it is in the name of Thy Son, our Saviour, Jesus Christ, we ask it. Amen."

Now it was June's turn. Unlike me, she seemed at ease in the atmosphere of worship.

"Dear heavenly Father, forgive me my sins," she calmly implored. "Help me not to envy my neighbor's possessions or her . . . things."

I knew what this referred to. Her best friend had just been given a formal dress for a school dance; June wanted one like it, but had been refused.

Suddenly I realized that this was no time to be listening to my sister. In a few moments she would be through, and it would be my turn. What would I pray about? What were the words, the tricks of expression, the archaic language with which to achieve a semblance of piety? I had nothing to say to God and would have liked to forego my turn. What would happen, I wondered, if I should say, "Excuse me, please"? Something terrible. Better to patch together an artifact of reverence and speak to the Lord, not from the heart, but from the necessity of circumstance. God, I knew, could distinguish the sincere from the merely professed; but this did not concern me. My efforts were directed toward meeting only those requirements imposed by my earthly father.

What, then, could I say? It was always proper to ask forgiveness for my sins, to ask God's blessing and mercy, and to pray that my father get well. But this could be said very quickly. It was not long enough. I could ask God to make me good, not only in word and deed but also in thought. That was an old one, but still worth using. I could pray, also, that I be less quick to anger and more willing to forgive those who sinned against me. I could hardly have named a vice from which I was more nearly free than that of losing my temper, and I would have been hard put to name a person who had sinned against me; but it was easier to compose a prayer in clichés than with real sins, shortcomings, and needs. I could ask also that . . .

But it was too late now! June was about to finish. Something in the tone of her voice told me that the sentence now being spoken would be her last, that it would end with the words . . . yes, there they were:

". . . in the name of our Lord, Jesus Christ, Amen."

The room became quiet. They were waiting for me. There was no getting out of it.

"Dear Lord," I began nervously, "Forgive us our sins." Here in the house of my everyday life I was standing on my knees with my face in my hands. In a lighted room I had closed my eyes. Having nothing to say, I was speaking insincere words in obsolete phrases to an unseen presence. "Make us to understand Thy meaning and know Thy way"—this had not been planned; it just came out—"and follow Thy path. Help us to forgive our enemies and be kind to those who have sinned against us. Let us be slow to anger, O Lord, and"—strange how much easier it was once in the swing of it—"let us always strive to be like our Lord and Saviour, Jesus Christ. Give us strength when temptation comes, and help us to do the right thing. Make us good, not only in word and deed but also in thought. Bless Daddy, dear Lord, and make him well. And bless Mama and June, and make me a better boy, for Christ's sake, Amen."

It was a great relief to have finished, and it was a pretty good prayer, I thought. At least I had not troubled the Almighty with such matters as a new dress.

Now the family's most gifted solicitor of heaven began to speak.

"Lord God in heaven, Thou who art so sadly familiar with our misdeeds and limitations, Thou who doth weep when even the least of us doth forsake Thy way and embrace evil, Thou who . . . "

This voice which, despite invalidism, was forceful and resonant, reverent without being humble, never failed to awe me. I felt that Daddy was closer to God than the rest of us, conversant with Him on more nearly equal terms.

" . . . look Thou down upon the miserable shambles of our sin-wrecked lives, O Lord, and be Thou not unmoved by our plight, but let Thy . . . "

With the familiar thunder of this rhetoric in my ears, I could now relax. I could dream or doze or listen, as I chose. Surreptitiously I lowered my rump onto my heels. Such a posture was not permitted at worship; but probably Daddy could not see me. Anyway, I would take the chance.

" . . . purify our hearts with the flame of Thy righteous anger, O God. Spare not Thy rod, but use it to show us Thy way. . . ."

I opened my eyes and looked out narrowly between my fingers. By turning my head slightly, I could see Mama's legs extended behind her. They were covered with wrinkled cotton stockings of a tan color. The sole of her right shoe was worn through to the lining, and suddenly this seemed unaccountably pathetic. I thought of her only as being on her feet—coming, going, serving, working—it was strange to see her in this position, her legs splayed out unnaturally on the floor, the soles of her shoes turned upward, as though she had been injured by violence and were lying unconscious.

" . . . Forsake us not in our misdeeds. Be with us always. Let Thy presence be ever felt in our hearts, a beacon in the night of our unworthiness. . . ."

Daddy's voice rose and fell, giving me a sense of security even though I did not listen.

" . . . Purge our minds of evil thoughts. . . . Inscribe on the tables of our hearts . . . "

Near at hand was my sister, her dark brown hair hanging over her shoulders. She wore a sleeveless nightgown, and I could see a curve of breast. I felt a vague stirring of desire and unrest.

" . . . to us. Bless this family, Thou who knowest all our wants and needs. Grant our just and righteous hopes. Rid us of all designs unworthy of Thy favor. Bring back to us . . . "

I became absorbed in looking toward the light with my hands over my eyes, seeing through my fingers. They were red and translucent, like apple jelly.

"And if it be Thy will, O Lord, restore my health. . . ."

With our eyes covered, our thoughts following different paths, the family knelt and prayed; and outside the wind moved aimlessly across vast plains.

" . . . For Thine is the kingdom, the power and the glory, for ever and ever, Amen."

I AM BEING given a second chance. The gun is in my hands! Again my father tells me how to hold it, how to aim, how to fire; again sends me outside to await instructions; again assigns to me a sparrow. I take aim, and this time I am deadly serious, am determined not to lose this gun again. I want desperately to be a good shot, like my father, want him to be proud of me. With my left hand I steady the barrel against the corner of the house. I take aim. Then I close my eyes, whisper, "Dear God, help me to kill this sparrow. Bless Daddy and Mama, and make Daddy well, and help me be a good boy and do Thy will, and please God help me not to shake, dear God, and help me kill this sparrow. Amen." I open my eyes, the bird is still there. This time I won't be hurried, I'm going to do this right. The tip of the front sight on the sparrow's heart is barely visible in the bottom of the V. I squeeze the trigger, the sparrow falls. I am startled, a little surprised, didn't think I could do it. Delight spreads through me. I wait for commendation from above, but Daddy says nothing. After a while another sparrow appears and I am given my assignment. Again the sparrow falls. Now I am exultant, invincible, anointed. I am my father's son.

I kill five birds without a miss before I am called inside. This time, standing straight before my father, I surrender the rifle gladly, knowing I have earned the right to get it back. My father looks at me in silence, his face relaxed, comfortable, the face I love and seldom see. I know he is proud of me. I am bursting with triumph, jubilation, excitement, the world opening before me.

"That was good shooting," he says easily.

My face is burning, I look at the floor.

"Last time you couldn't hit anything; this time you didn't miss. Think over what you have just done, and tell me how you did it. I don't want you to lose what you have just learned. You understand?"

"Yes, sir."

"So, tell me. What did you do this time that was different?"

I look up confidently, knowing my answer will please him. "This time, before each shot, I prayed to God, asked Him to help me kill the sparrow."

He did not respond. A strange expression took over his face. His gaze released me, turned inward.

ON ANY SUNDAY morning in summer a congregation of fifty to seventy-five would sit on the uncomfortable benches of our country church in the withering heat and listen to the sermon; and one of them, much against his will, was always me. The beginning of the service was a tiresome miscellany: reading of the text, collection of the offering, announcements, and the meaningless dialogue of responsive reading. The succession of these items was punctuated by rising and the singing of hymns. Sometimes I would sing loudly, causing my mother to

nudge me, or, if that were to no avail, to whisper exasperated-
ly that I was "not to lead the singing." Most of the time, however, I would be silent, and watch the others, or stare moodily
at nothing at all. After about fifteen minutes the preliminaries
would be finished, and everyone would settle back to listen to
the sermon. Occasionally I would pay attention for a while,
particularly if an anecdote were being related. Sometimes I
would even be moved. But for the most part I mused about
indifferent matters, perhaps counting the holes in the roof
through which I could see daylight. Every five or ten minutes
I would ask Mama if the sermon were about over, and she
would whisper: "Yes, just a little while longer. Now be quiet."

On and on the sermon would drone and meander, or, if the
minister were of the choleric type, would proceed explosively.
I would wait . . . and wait . . . and hope for an ending until it
would seem I had been sitting there always and that the sermon would go on forever. I would want to slip down on the
bench so as to rest my head against the back, but that was forbidden. Nor could I draw up my feet and sit cross-legged, nor
lean on my mother's shoulder. Eventually I would despair and
subside into a trance. With my neck constricted by a tight collar, my metabolism confounded by the heat, the inactivity, and
the exhortation, I would become dizzy and see things spin
before my eyes. Realizing that this perversion of vision could
be ended by an effort of will, I would not wish to end it, but
would be amused and would preserve it. Now I could see the
preacher sail rapidly through the air, still gesticulating, and
disappear out of the window. And all of the people and benches would sail out after him. With further relaxation of my eye
muscles I could see two preachers go sailing by.

If at such a moment Mama should glance at me she would
be chagrined to see my head wagging, my mouth open, my
eyes rolling, and a silly grin on my face. Thinking that I was
making faces at the minister, she would nudge me sharply and

whisper an angry reprimand. I would come out of my daze and the waiting would continue.

Once more I would ask if the sermon were almost finished, and she would purse her lips in displeasure and refuse to answer. I would make an effort to sit still and attend, but after a few minutes would lose the train of thought. Then I would scratch my head and inadvertently touch my ear and that would start me off again. As though previously unaware of this appendage, I would begin to explore it, sticking my fingers into its orifice, following out each groove, and comparing it with the one on the opposite side. Next, I might try to wiggle them. A stern glance from my mother would inform me that I was again misbehaving. Feeling that the world was united in solid conspiracy against me, I would try once more to sit still.

Finally I would hear the long-awaited words: "Now let us kneel in prayer."

Getting down on my knees would revive me and renew my hope. After the prayer the congregation would resume its seats, the choir leader would step forward and announce the hymn, and all would stand to sing. Finally came the benediction, the shortest and most satisfactory thing ever said in church. With eyes closed and arms outstretched, palms down, the minister would intone: "Now may the grace of God be with you all till we meet again. Amen."

The problem then was getting out of the church. Alone, this could have been accomplished at once; but with my mother it took some time. No sooner were we in the aisle than she would greet someone, shake hands, comment on the sermon, ask about the other's family, and answer queries about her own. This would be repeated many times as we gradually made our way toward the altar. There, after standing and chatting for a while, she would manage to reach Brother Gibson and would tell him that his sermon was an "inspiring message." The pastor would clasp her hand warmly in both of his and hold it for some time, shaking it intermittently. He would ask about Daddy, about June, and would beam down on me and say jovially, "Well, how's this little man?"

"All right, sir."

We would not stay long with the pastor, as others would be waiting to speak to him. We would begin then the long trek toward the exit, making poor headway because of frequent stops. In a brief interval between encounters I would plead, "Mama, please let's go on home now!"

And she would reply absently, "All right, hon, we'll go right away."

Someone would then again detain us to chat. After ten or fifteen minutes we would be outside the church, and there the diminishing group would stand and talk a while longer. This was the only social life my mother had, but I did not think of that, was only exasperated by the delay. When at last we would start off together toward home in the glaring heat, we would be tired and hot and thirsty.

Now, however, there was a fine thing to look forward to. On arriving home I would drink a glass of water and, unless my father detained me with questions about the Sunday School lesson, would begin reading the funny papers. Lying prone on the living-room floor, I would study them with great care, would read the dialogue and minutely examine each illustration before going on to the next frame. However tempted, I would not look ahead to discover the ending first. I relished each word and each picture, prolonging its pleasure as long as possible, and this would occupy me for about an hour. The next hour would be given over to Sunday dinner, the best meal of the week. When this was over I would dry the dishes as June washed them.

Then I would experience a feeling that was to remain with me always—the emptiness and loneliness of Sunday afternoons. It was a feeling that came on gradually. For a while after dinner I would be fairly content, musing over the funny papers, or perhaps reading them again, but soon would feel the beginning of unrest. I would walk through the house, stopping in front of windows and staring moodily outside. Sometimes I would go out and walk around, as if looking for something I knew was not there, then come in again, my loneliness increased. Passing the piano, I would wish I could play, would softly touch the keys. Searching out my mother and sister, I would find them engaged in activities alien to my unknown desires.

"Mama, what can I do?" I would ask sadly.

"Well, hon, let me see . . . Why don't you read a book?" Seeing my face unchanged, she might add, "Or why don't you get June to play dominoes with you?"

I didn't want to read, June didn't want to play dominoes, and Mama had no more suggestions. There was nothing to do on Sunday. If any of my friends had come to see me, I would have been permitted to play some quiet game with them, but they did not come. Their families were not so devout, and they were not interested in quiet games. I was not permitted to visit them; I had to stay within the house or its immediate environs. Nor was I allowed to put on old clothes so as to be able to crawl under the house or dig a cave or climb a tree. Sunday was a day for rest and quiet relaxation. But rest I did not need, the silence was already too much, and relaxation impossible within the limits imposed.

Having ascertained that, as I supposed, no escape was possible, I would act on my mother's suggestion and look for a book. Approaching the bookcase, I would stare morosely at the row of titles behind the glass door. I was familiar with most of them because of similar experiences on past Sundays. Although I had read only a few, I had tried them all and found them dull. The volume to which I most frequently returned was Dante's *Divine Comedy*, which showed little evidence of ever having been read. There was, however, much to recommend it. I had heard my mother say it was a great book; I knew that comedy was what I most liked; and a divine comedy could hardly be anything other than a superlatively funny one. So it was usually Dante's work I eventually drew from the bookcase. I had long since given up on starting at the beginning. I had tried that many times, and there was certainly nothing funny on the first few pages. It was a long book, though; and, assuming that the really funny parts came later, I would thumb through the pages, reading a bit here and there, never finding the fun for which I was looking. Not in all the Sundays of my youth did I discover Dante's concealed hilarity, and gradually the book became a symbol of the desolate day itself.

Having confirmed my belief that the bookcase contained nothing of interest, I would again wander through the house, or perhaps curl up in a chair and daydream. The world, I knew, was full of adventure and fun and friendship, if only I were free to find them. Someday, I promised myself, I would be free. Then I would do as I liked, search and find, and never be lonely again. Thus would pass the afternoon of the seventh day.

Supper consisted of what was left over from dinner, and was eaten cold in the quiet kitchen. If Daddy were feeling bad we would stay home; but if Mama thought he could spare her, she would again go to church and I would be obliged to go with her. Together we would set out just before dark.

The evening service was much like that of the morning, except shorter, more informal, and attended by fewer people. There was, however, a great difference in my attitude toward it. The funny papers had been read, the day was over, and there was nothing to look forward to. Only loneliness remained. I was not tempted to misbehave and would sit quietly through the sermon, sometimes listening to what Brother Gibson said, but for the most part hearing the voice only of my own desire.

My feelings would merge with those of the songs we sang. All hymns were sad and seemed even more so when sung at night by a small congregation in a country church. Looking at the people around me, I would think of all of them as being middle-aged or old, and would suspect that all of them were unhappy. The men were carpenters, plumbers, postmen, grocers, trolley-car operators, insurance salesmen, and invalided veterans of the war. The women were housewives. Of what, I would wonder, were they thinking as they stood and sang these sad songs. Perhaps of the routine of work to begin again tomorrow. Perhaps of the failure of plans and hopes. The sound of their voices suggested that they had come here to pool their loneliness, to reaffirm their membership in a group, and to be told that all their hardships were manifestations of God's inscrutable plan and that their lives were somehow converging toward an end of eternal happiness.

Sometimes I would glance obliquely at my mother and see her face stroked with sadness as she sang the mournful hymns in a high, sweet voice, always slightly off-key:

> Where He leads me I will follow,
> Where He leads me I will follow,
> Where He leads me I will follow,
> I'll go with Him, with Him,
> All the way.

As we walked back home in silence through the still night, no light for our steps but the stars, I would resolve to make my life different from those I had seen, to have my happiness here on this earth. I believed that this was possible.

When I was seven my father improved, blood disappeared from his sputum, he was in high spirits, was getting well. For the first time I saw him up and about, in ordinary clothes. My mother was blooming. Foreboding drained from her face, color rushed in, she had never been so pretty. My father bought a Maxwell touring car, we went driving through the countryside, and when it rained we snapped on the isinglass window curtains. It was about this time, too, my mother agreed to call Tall Betsy.

Tall Betsy was perhaps eight feet tall, with long, willowy arms. No one had ever seen her face. From the top of her head to the ground she was clothed in trailing white robes. She did not speak, but uttered wailing cries and sharp growls. Sometimes on a cold, windy night I would hear from far away a sound such as might be made by a woman in pain, and would start up with alarm. "What's that?" And my mother would answer, "That's Tall Betsy," and I would wait anxiously for the cry to be repeated. Sometimes I would ask, "Mama, doesn't she get cold out there in the woods?" And my mother would answer confidently, "No, she doesn't mind the cold in winter or the heat in summer."

Tall Betsy had never been seen except at night; no one knew where she stayed by day. Very likely, I thought, she made herself invisible or changed into a stump. I had often looked for her in caves or gullies or hollow trees, both longing to find her and relieved I did not. Sometimes at night, however, she would come out of the woods, and even enter our yard. Apparently my mother had an understanding with her; for when my mother called she would come. Tall Betsy, my father once said, roamed all over the world, but loved my mother with a pure and ghostly love, and no matter how far away she might be—even in China—she would always come when my mother called.

But Tall Betsy was more than a ghost, and more than a game, she was also a threat, a lurking menace, an unbearable loss. For if, when my mother was exhausted and harassed, I added to her strain and her troubles by importuning or misbehaving, her patience would crack, and she would cry out, "I can't stand it any longer! I just can't! I can't! I'm going away to the woods and live with Tall Betsy!" And a spiraling pain would twist down in my heart.

Dinner is over, my father is polishing the Maxwell, I am helping my mother with the dishes. I am eager for her to be finished, for she has already agreed to call Tall Betsy. Bill Evans calls from the front of the house. Soon other children arrive. Bob Johnson, the two Miller boys with their dog, Sarge, and others. We sit on the porch in the twilight and talk in hushed tones, speculate about the creature we are about to see. Is she a ghost or just an old woman who lives in the woods? As dusk changes to night we become tense and expectant, the younger boys glancing apprehensively at the edge of the woods about fifty yards away. Sarge howls, and a shiver passes through us. Bob says he once saw Tall Betsy in the daytime, but Tom Evans says no, that she can't be seen in daylight. I then tell them (making it up as I go along) that my father said that Tall Betsy once carried off a little boy, and the whole town searched the woods for weeks, but no trace was ever found; it stands to reason, then, that if Tall Betsy gets hold of you, "you are a goner."

After a while my mother comes out with a lamp and sits on the porch with us. We beg her to call right away, but she says we must wait, that Tall Betsy never comes before dark. We ply her with questions; her answers are cryptic and evasive. We must not approach too closely, we are not to throw stones. Tom volunteers that if you do, Tall Betsy will set your house on fire.

Night has come now. There are ten of us sitting on the steps, waiting. We become quiet and listen intently. The hum of crickets and the croaking of frogs are the only sounds. The blackness of night is sequined with fireflies.

"Call her now, Mama!"

"All right. But she may not come, you know." She walks out

in the darkness where she is visible to us only as a blur. We marvel at her bravery. As for ourselves, we stay near the porch, so we can run into the house if Tall Betsy comes too close. When my mother reaches the woods she stops and in a high voice begins to call:

"Tall . . . ll . . . Bet . . . sy!"

We are tensely quiet, we look about. No telling where she might appear. Perhaps right beside us. Minutes pass. No one speaks. The silence and uncertainty build such suspense that we are ready, equally, to laugh or run or cry. After a while my mother tries again. A high-pitched, tremulous, singing call:

"Tall . . . ll . . . Bet . . . sy!"

Again we wait, half in hope, half in fear, my mother's plaintive call lingering in the air. When another span of foreboding silence has passed, someone says, "Maybe she won't come." But just as we begin to breathe easier, we are chilled by a manic cry.

"That's her! That's Tall Betsy!" I shout.

"Where? Where is she? I don't see her."

"I don't know," I say, "but that was her all right! She made that sound!"

We look in all directions, see nothing. As the waiting continues, some of the more daring venture away from the house, among them me. I feel that, in a sense, it is my game, it belongs to me, and so am determined to play a major part. Presently one of us sees what all are looking for.

"There she is! By that tree!"

"That white thing?"

"Yes, that's her!"

"It's not moving."

"It moved just a minute ago. That's her all right." Then a long, lonely wailing.

"There! That's where it came from!"

"Look! It's moving!"

"That's her! That's Tall Betsy!"

At first we see only a white haze, which, as we watch, slowly approaches. We group together, watch in silence. All are afraid. She is the tallest living thing we ever have seen, as tall as the mesquite trees from which she eerily emerges. Her arms are proportionately long, and she waves them in a sinuous, uncanny motion. No one can see her face, or indeed, even know that she has one. She seems to consist entirely of flowing white drapery. Her approach takes a long time, for she weaves slowly back and forth, occasionally emitting the awful cry. As there seems to be no immediate danger, I compose myself sufficiently to call out, "Hey! Tall Betsy! I'm not afraid of you!" On being so addressed, she stops, growls, takes a few quick steps in our direction. There is a sharp intake of breath among us.

"If you are not afraid," Bob says, "why don't you go on out there?"

"All right, I will. Come get me, Tall Betsy. I'm not afraid of you!"

The apparition growls again and makes a dash for me. The girls shriek, the boys laugh nervously, and the group breaks up, everyone running and yelling in excitement. One of us provokes her to give chase and then flees, laughing and screaming, until someone else can command her attention and malice.

"I bet you can't catch me, Tall Betsy!"

"I'm not afraid of any old ghost!"

"I could lick ten Tall Betsys!"

"You'd better not set my house on fire. I'll beat the tar out of you!"

"Don't catch me, Tall Betsy. I'll kick you in the pants!"

Yet all of us run when she gives chase.

Presently, as I am standing in the outer fringe of the group, resting from a sortie, Tall Betsy suddenly, without warning or provocation, singles me out. She points her long arm, growls, and dashes for me. I turn and flee, escaping her grasp, but to my dismay find that she is between me and the house. Unable to elude her by running to either side, I am forced to enter the woods, and there, in the blackness, out of sight of the house, I am terrified. Stumbling, in panic, scratched by thorns, I manage to escape her, come upon a back road, and reach home from a different direction. There I find that Tall Betsy has returned and that the game is going on without me. Forced to sit down to rest and compose myself, I resolve to be more cautious.

It was wonderful fun, being chased by a spook, and we could have played it all night. Tall Betsy tires of it, however; after an hour of snarling and chasing she begins to retreat, weaving and swaying in her ghostly fashion. And as she moves further from the lamp on the porch we become less willing to go near her. When she reaches the woods, she makes beckoning gestures to my mother. Having ignored her throughout the game, she now seems eager that my mother come to her.

"Look!" Tom says. "She's signaling!"

"What's she trying to do?"

"Allen's mother is going to her!"

"She's hypnotized!"

My mother responds hesitantly, approaching a few steps at a time. While the others watch with interest, I watch with alarm.

"Mama!" She stops and looks back wonderingly. "Mama! Come back!"

As if weighing the two invitations, she looks again at Tall Betsy, whose gestures have become more imperative.

"Mama! . . . Mama! Come back!"

With a last look at me she yields to the wraith, goes forward until Tall Betsy's long arm reaches out and takes her hand.

"Mama!" I cry.

Now she does not look back. The two slowly enter the woods. In desperation I run to them and catch my mother's free hand in both my own. The closeness to Tall Betsy terrifies me, but the thought of losing my mother is unbearable. Trying to keep her between me and Tall Betsy, I pull on her arm and plead, "Mama! Come back!"

As if in a trance she stops, turns to me, and says, "Tall Betsy wants me to go away to the woods and live with her."

"Don't go, Mama! Don't go. Please!"

As my mother stands there undecided, Tall Betsy becomes impatient and tries to drag her. I hold firm, and no progress is made. Irritated by my opposition, the ghost snarls and flails at me. I try to dodge the unnaturally long arms while clinging desperately to my mother and trying to draw her away. "Mama! *Please!*"

"Well . . . I don't know."

"Mama!" I scream, my voice cracking.

She squeezes my hand. "All right, hon. Don't cry." Then, to the ghost, she says, "I guess I can't go with you tonight."

Tall Betsy receives this with a spasm of anger, but my mother and I begin walking back toward the house. I keep looking over my shoulder in case we should be pursued and hold tight to my mother lest she change her mind. Ignoring the curious glances of the other children, I hold on to her hand long after we reach the porch, to be sure she stays.

For a while longer Tall Betsy can be seen weaving about in the edge of the woods, now appearing, now disappearing, while we sit on the steps and watch. Finally she disappears entirely, but still for a while we hear her cry, gradually becoming more distant. When heard no more, the game is over and the other children begin, apprehensively, reluctantly, to leave. They depart in groups, staying close together and in the middle of the road.

When all are gone, my mother and I enter the house. My

father is sitting in the kitchen by a lamp, breathing heavily. Sweat stands out on his face.

"Daddy," I say excitedly, "you should have come out. Tall Betsy almost pulled Mama away into the woods!"

He does not reply, and there is something in his expression that makes me fall silent. Mama sits down across the room from him, I by her side.

"Well . . . " she says, but there is no response and she does not continue.

She holds me close and strokes my hair. I am uncomfortable looking at my father, hide my face on her shoulder. A heavy silence hangs in the room.

MY FATHER'S RECOVERY proved but a brief remission. Within a month the racking cough returned, and the bloody sputum. He sold the Maxwell, fell back in bed, back in pajamas, resumed the downward slide of tuberculosis.

I AM SEVEN years old; the other boys range up to thirteen. We are playing baseball on stony ground near my house. I am at shortstop. A hard-hitter sends the ball flashing toward me; I put out a glove, but flinch; the ball strikes a stone, whizzes by. I am running ashamedly after it when I hear my father call my name. A harsh, stentorian summons. I go to the house, stand below the window of his sickroom.

"I will not permit a son of mine to be a coward!" The voice throbs with fury, with contempt, outrage. "When a ball comes at you like that, you *stand in the way.* If you can't catch it in your glove, you *stop it with your body!* Now you get back out there and don't you ever let me see you do that again!"

At the very center of me, he taught me, was something craven. A softness that made the knees weak. A maternal protectiveness of self, instead of daring and disregard. The stuff of which I was made was fear; the right stuff was courage. Life became a denying of what I was while trying to become something I was not. The real me must never be seen.

IT WAS THE last day of school. The report cards had been distributed, and—to my great relief—I had passed. Now at eleven o'clock in the morning I was on my way home with two friends. We felt exhilaration at the prospect of three months of freedom and manifested it by pushing each other, yelling, throwing rocks at a bottle, chasing a grass snake, and rolling a log into the creek. Being eight years old, it took us a long time to get home. Before parting, we made plans to meet in the afternoon to play ball. I ran through the tall grass up to the back door and into the kitchen. My mother was stirring something on the stove.

"Mama, I passed!"

"Not so loud, hon." She leaned over and kissed me, then looked at the report card. "This is very good. Show it to Daddy if he's not asleep."

I went through the bedroom to the glassed-in porch. The bed faced away from the door and I could not tell whether he was asleep or not.

"Daddy?"

"Come in, son."

"I passed," I said, offering the card.

He smiled and I lowered my eyes. I could never bring myself to face for long the level gaze of those pale blue eyes, which seemed effortlessly to read my mind. He looked over the report. "I see you got seventy-five in conduct."

"Yes, sir."

"Do you have an explanation?"

"No, sir."

"Do you think you deserved a better grade?"

"No . . . sir."

"Then you *do* have an explanation?"

I twisted one foot around the other. "Yes, sir. I guess so, sir."

"What is the explanation?"

This tireless interrogation could, I knew, be carried on for hours. Mumbling the words, I began to recount my sins. "I guess I . . . talked too much."

"Speak up, son."

"Yes, sir. I talked too much . . . and laughed . . . and cut up."

"Do you find silence so difficult?"

"Sir?"

"Was it so hard to be quiet?"

"Yes . . . sir. I guess so."

"You don't seem to find it difficult now."

I looked up and found him smiling. It wasn't going to be so bad after all. "But the other grades are good," he said. I grinned and turned to look out the window. Heat waves shimmered over the tin roof of the barn; away to the west was an unbroken field of sunflowers. Everything was bathed in, and seemed to be made drowsy by, the hot, bright sunlight. I thought of playing ball and wished dinner were over so I could go now.

"Daddy, can I go over to Paul's house after dinner?" Almost before the words were out, I realized my mistake. I should have asked my mother first. She might have said yes without consulting my father.

"No. You have to work, son."

"What've I got to do?"

He looked out over the several acres which we called the backyard. "You have to cut the grass."

Through a long, wet spring the grass had sprung up until it was nearly a foot high. Now, in June, the rain was over and the heat was beginning to turn the grass brown. As we had no lawn mower, any cutting of grass or weeds was done by hoe, scythe, or sickle. It was with one of these, I assumed, that the grass would be cut, but I was mistaken. After dinner my father gave me directions. The tool was to be an old, ivory-handled, straight-edge razor. The method was to grasp a handful of grass in the left hand and cut it level with the ground with the razor. The cut grass was to be put in a basket, along with any rocks or sticks that might be found on the ground. When the basket was full, it was to be removed some fifty yards where the grass could be emptied and burned. When the razor was dull it was to be sharpened on a whetstone in the barn.

I changed my clothes, put on a straw hat, and went to work. Unable to realize the extent of the task or to gauge the time required, my only thought was to finish as soon as possible so as to be able to play before the afternoon was over. I began in the center of the yard and could see my father watching from his bed on the porch. After a few experimental slashes an idea occurred to me. I walked to the house and stood under the windows of the porch.

"Daddy."

"Yes, son."

"When I've finished, can I play baseball?"

"Yes."

I resumed work, thinking I would cut fast and get it done in a couple of hours. For a few minutes all went well; there was some satisfaction in watching the thin steel cut easily through dry grass. I grabbed big handfuls and hacked away with gusto. Soon my father called. Obediently I walked to the porch. "Yes, sir?" He was looking through field glasses at the small patch of ground that had been cleared.

"Son, I want you to cut the grass *level* with the ground. Therefore you will have to cut slower and more carefully. Take a smaller handful at a time so you can cut it evenly. Also, you must pick up every stone." This referred to the few pebbles left in the cleared area. "Do you understand?"

"Yes, sir."

"Now go back and do that patch over again, and cut it level with the ground."

"Yes, sir."

Walking back, I wondered why I had not started in some part of the yard out of my father's view. The work was now harder; for the stubble was only one or two inches high and was difficult to hold while being cut. It took an hour to do again the area originally cleared in a few minutes. By this time I was tired and disheartened. Sweat ran down my forehead and into my eyes; my mouth was dry. The razor could not be held by the handle, for the blade would fold back. It had to be held by its narrow shank, which already had raised a blister.

Presently I heard my friends, who then came into view and approached the fence.

"Whatya doin'?"

"Cuttin' the grass."

"What's that you're cuttin' it with?"

"A razor."

They laughed. "That's a funny thing to be cuttin' grass with."

"Son!" The boys stopped laughing and I went to the porch.

"Yes, sir?"

"If you want to talk to your friends, you may; but don't stop working while you talk."

"Yes, sir." I went back to the basket and resumed cutting.

"What'd he say?" Paul asked in a lowered voice.

"He said I had to work."

"You can't play ball?"

"No."

"How long is he going to make you work?"

"I don't know."

"Well—I guess we might as well go on."

I looked up with longing. They were standing outside the fence, poking their toes idly through the palings. James was

rhythmically pounding his fist into the socket of a first base-
man's mitt.

"Yeah, let's get goin'."

"Can you get away later on?" Paul asked.

"Maybe I can. I'll try. I'll see if he'll let me." The two boys
began to wander off. "I'll try to come later," I called urgently,
hoping my father would not hear.

When they were gone I tried for a while to cut faster, but my
hand hurt. Several times I had struck rocks with the razor, and
the blade was getting dull. Gingerly I got up from my sore
knees, went to the hydrant, allowed the water to run until cool,
and drank from my cupped hands. Then I went to the barn
and began whetting the blade on the stone. When it was sharp,
I sat down to rest. Being out of my father's sight I felt relatively safe for the moment. The chinaberry tree cast a liquid pattern of sun and shade before the door. The berries were green
and firm, just right for a slingshot.

"Son!"

With a sense of guilt I hurried to my father's window. "Yes,
sir."

"Get back to work. It's not time to rest yet."

At midafternoon I looked about and saw how little I had
done. Heat waves shimmered before my eyes and I realized
that I would not finish today and perhaps not tomorrow.
Leaving the razor on the ground, I made the familiar trek to
my father's window.

"Daddy."

"Yes."

"Can I quit now?"

"No, son."

"I can't finish it this afternoon."

"I know."

"Then can't I go play ball now and finish it tomorrow?"

"No."

"When can I play ball?"

"When you have finished cutting the grass."

"How long do you think it'll take me?"

"Two or three months."

"Well, can . . . ?"

"Now that's enough. Go back to work."

I resumed work at a sullenly slow pace. To spare my knees I sat down, cutting around me as far as I could reach, then moving to a new place and sitting down again.

"Son!"

I went back to the porch. "Yes, sir."

"Do you want to be a lazy, no-account scoundrel?" The voice was harsh and angry.

"No, sir."

"Then don't you ever let me see you sitting down to work again! Now you get back out there as quick as you can and *stand on your knees!*"

The afternoon wore on with excruciating slowness. The sun gradually declined. The thin shank of the razor cut into my hand and the blisters broke. I showed them to my father, hoping they would prove incapacitating, but he bandaged them and sent me back. Near sundown I heard the sounds of my friends returning to their homes, but they did not come by to talk. Finally my mother came to the back door, said supper was ready. The day's work was over.

WHEN I WOKE the next morning I thought it was another school day, then remembered the preceding afternoon and knew that school was far better than cutting grass. I knew that my father intended for me to continue the work, but as no specific order had been given for this particular day, there was possibility of escape. I decided to ask my mother for permission to play, and to be gone before my father realized what had happened.

My mother was cooking breakfast when I finished dressing. I made myself useful and waited until, for some reason, she went out on the back porch. Now we were separated from my father by three rooms and clearly out of earshot.

"Mama, can I go over to Paul's house?"

"Why yes, hon, I guess so."

That was my mother. To the reasonable request she said yes immediately; the unreasonable required a varying amount of cajolery, but in the end that too would be granted. When breakfast was over, I quickly got my cap, whispered a soft good-bye, and started out. I had reached the back door when she called, "Be sure you come back before dinner."

"Son!"

I stopped. In another moment I would have been far enough away to pretend I had not heard. But though my conscience might be deaf to a small voice, it was not deaf to this sternly audible one. If I ran now, I would never be able to look at my father and say, "No, I didn't hear you." I gave my mother a reproachful glance as I went back through the kitchen. "Now I won't get to go," I said darkly.

I entered the glass porch and stood by the bed, eyes lowered. I was aware of omitting the required "Yes, sir," but did not care.

"Where were you off to?"

"To Paul's."

"Who told you you could go?"

"Mama."

"Did you ask her?"

"Yes."

"Yes what?"

"Yes, sir," I said sulkily.

"Didn't you know I wanted you to work today?"

"No, sir."

"Don't you remember my telling you that you could not play until you finished cutting the grass?"

"No, sir." One lie followed another now. "Anyway . . . that will take just about . . . all summer." My mouth was dry and I was swallowing heavily. "James and Paul don't have to work and . . . I don't see why . . . I . . . have to work all the time."

I choked, my eyes burned, and tears were just one harsh word away. After a moment I saw the covers of the bed move; my father's long, wasted legs appeared. The tears broke, flooding my face. My father stood up, slowly, with difficulty, found his slippers, put on a bathrobe. My ear was seized and twisted by a bony hand, and I was propelled into the bathroom. My father sat on the edge of the tub and held me in front of him. The fingers were relentless, and it seemed that my ear would be torn from my head.

"Look at me, son."

Tears were dripping from my chin, and every other moment my chest was convulsed by a rattling sob. Trying to stop crying, I managed at last to raise my head and look in my father's face. The head and neck were thin. The skin had a grayish glint, and the lines that ran down from his nose were straight. His eyes were steady, and on their level, searching gaze my conscience was impaled.

"Do you know why you are going to be punished?"

The pose of injured innocence was gone now. My guilt seemed everywhere, there was no place to hide.

"Yes . . . sir."

"Why?"

"Because . . . I . . . didn't tell the . . . truth." It was terrible to look into those eyes.

"And?" The question was clipped and hard.

"And . . . because. . . ."

I tried to search my conscience and enumerate my sins, but my mind was a shambles and my past was mountainous with guilt. I could not speak. My eyes dropped.

"Look at me, son."

It was agony to lift my eyes again to that knifelike gaze, that implacable accusation.

"You are being punished because you tried to get your mother's permission for an act you knew to be wrong. You were scoundrel enough to do that!" the razored voice said. "Do you understand?"

"Yes . . . sir."

"You are being punished, further, because you were sullen and insubordinate. Do you understand?"

"Yes . . . sir."

I saw the other hand move and felt the old, sick terror. The hand grasped the clothes of my back and lifted me onto my father's knees. My head hung down to the floor. The hand began to rise and fall.

"Do you understand why you're being punished?"

"Ye-es . . . sir."

The blows were heavy and I cried out.

"Will you ever do any of those things again?"

"No . . . sir."

The whipping lasted about a minute, after which I was placed on my feet. "Now, stop crying and wash your face. Then go out in the yard to work."

Still sobbing, I approached the lavatory, turned on a trickle of water. Behind me I heard my father stand and slowly leave the room. I held both hands under the faucet, stared with unseeing eyes at the drops of water tumbling over my fingers. Gradually the sobs diminished. I washed my face and left the room, closing the door softly. Passing through the kitchen I was aware that my mother was looking at me with compassion, but I avoided her eyes. To look at her now would be to cry again.

All that day I worked steadily and quietly, asked no questions, made no requests. The work was an expiation and my father found no occasion to criticize. Several times my mother brought out something cold for me to drink. She did not mention my punishment, but knowledge of it was eloquent in her eyes. In the afternoon I began to feel better and thought of my friends and of playing ball. Knowing it to be out of the question, I only dreamed about it.

That evening when supper was over and the dishes washed, my father called me.

"Tell him you're sorry," my mother whispered.

In our house after every punishment there had to be a reconciliation, the integrity of the bonds that held us had to be reaffirmed. Words of understanding had to be spoken, tokens of love given and received. I walked out on the porch. The sky was filled with masses of purple and red.

"Do you feel better now, son?"

"Yes, sir." The blue eyes contained a reflection of the sunset. "I'm sorry I acted the way I did this morning."

A hand was laid on my head. "You said you didn't know why you had to work, didn't you?"

"Yes, sir, but I . . . "

"That's all right, son. I'll tell you. You ought to know. When you are grown, you will have to work to make a living. All your life you'll have to work. Even if we were rich, you would labor, because idleness is sinful. The Bible tells us that. I hope some day you will be able to work with your head, but first you've got to know how to work with your hands." The color of the ponderous clouds was deepening to blue and black. "No one is born knowing how to work. It is something we have to learn. You've got to learn to set your mind to a job and keep at it, no matter how hard it is or how long it takes or how much you dislike it. If you don't learn that, you'll never amount to anything. And this is the time to learn it. Now, do you know why you have to cut the grass?"

"Yes, sir."

"I don't like to make you work when you want to play, but it's for your own good. Can you understand that?"

"Yes, sir."

"Will you be a good boy and work hard this summer until the job is done?"

"Yes, sir."

I left the room feeling better. It was good to be forgiven, to be on good terms with one's father.

DAY AFTER DAY I worked in the yard, standing on my knees, cutting the grass close to the ground. There were few interruptions to break the monotony. Three or four times a day I went to the barn and sharpened the razor, but these trips were no escape. If I went too often or stayed too long, my father took notice and put a stop to it. Many times each day I carried away the full basket of grass and stones, but the times of my departure and return were always observed. No evasions were possible because nothing escaped my father's eyes.

One day in July at noon I heard a rattle of dishes indicating that the table was being set. I was hot and tired and thirsty. I could smell the dinner cooking and thought of the tall glasses of iced tea. My mother came to the back door. At first I thought it was to call me, but it was only to throw out dishwater. Suddenly I dropped the razor and ran to the back steps.

"Mama," I called eagerly, but not loud enough for my father to hear. "Is dinner ready?"

"Yes, hon."

I came in, washed my hands, sat in the kitchen to wait.

"Son!"

It was my father's voice, the everlasting surveillance I could never escape.

"Yes, sir."

"What did you come in for?"

"Mama said dinner was ready."

"Did you *ask* her?"

"Yes, sir."

*Labeling him as the time
all back ... all*

"You trifling scoundrel! Get on back outside to work! And wait till she *calls* you to dinner! You understand?"

AS WEEKS PASSED, the heat increased and the grass withered. Had a match been touched to it, the work of a summer would have been accomplished in a few minutes. No rain fell, even for a day, to interrupt the work. The grass did not grow, and the ground which was cleared on the first day remained bare. The earth was baked to a depth of four or five feet and began to crack. The only living thing I encountered was an occasional spider climbing desperately in or out of the crevices in search of a habitable place. My friends knew I had to work and no longer came looking for me. Occasionally I would hear them playing in a nearby field, and sometimes in the mornings would see them pass with fishing poles over their shoulders. I knew that I was not missed, that they had stopped thinking of me and probably did not mention my name.

I became inured to the work but not reconciled to it, and throughout the summer continued to resist. Whippings—which had been rare before—were now common, and after each one I would, in the evening, be required to apologize. I would go out on my father's glass porch, say I was sorry, and listen guiltily to a restatement of the principles involved. Tirelessly my father would explain what I had done wrong, the importance of learning to work, and the benefit to my character that this discipline would eventually bring about. After each of these sessions I would feel that I was innately lazy and unworthy. I would resolve to try harder, and to overcome my resentment, but after two or three days I would again become sullen or rebellious and again would be punished. Sometimes I saw my mother in tears and knew she interceded in my behalf, but her efforts were ineffective.

THROUGHOUT JUNE AND July I worked every day except Sundays. As the job seemed endless I made no future plans. Anything that would last all summer was too large an obstacle to plan beyond, any happiness which lay at its end too remote to lift my spirit. About the middle of August, however, my outlook changed. One evening at sundown I noticed that relatively little grass remained standing. For the first time since the beginning of summer I realized that the job would have an end, that I would be free. Surveying the area remaining to be cut, I attempted to divide it by the area which could be cleared in a single day and reached an estimate of five days. I felt a surge of hope and began visualizing what I would do when I was through. During the next several days I worked faster and more willingly, but found that I had been too sanguine in my estimate. I did not finish on the fifth day or the sixth. But on the evening of the seventh, it was apparent to my father as well as to me that the next day the job would be done. Only one or two hours of work remained.

The following morning—for the first time since May—I woke to the sound of rain. I wanted to work anyway, to get it over, but was told I could not. Then I asked if I could go to Paul's house to play until the rain stopped. Again the answer was no. About nine o'clock the rain let up and I hurriedly began to work, but the lull was brief and after a few minutes I had to stop. I stood under the awning, which extended out over the windows of my father's porch, and waited. After a while I sat on the ground and leaned against the house. A half hour passed. The rain was steady now, seemingly would last all day. It dripped continuously from the canvas and formed a little trench in the earth in front of my feet. I stared out at the gray sky in a dull trance.

"I wish I could go to Paul's house."

I spoke in a low, sullen voice, hardly knowing whether I was talking to myself or to my father.

"It's not fair not to let me play . . . just because it's raining. It's not fair at all."

There was no comment from above. Minutes passed.

"You're a mean bastard!"

A feeling of strangeness swept over me. I had never cursed, was not used to such words. Something violent was stirring in me, something long stifled was rankling for expression.

"If you think you can kick me around all the time, you're wrong . . . you damned old bastard!"

At any moment I expected to be called. I would go inside then and receive a beating worse than I had known possible. A minute passed in silence.

Could it be that my father had not heard? That seemed unlikely, for always I spoke from this place and was always heard. The windows were open. There was nothing to prevent his hearing. Oh he had heard, all right. I was sure of that. Still, why wasn't I called? The waiting began to get on my nerves. Feeling that I could not make matters worse, I continued. This time I spoke louder and more viciously.

"You're the meanest man in the world. You lie up there in bed and are mean to everybody. I hate you!"

I began to feel astonished at myself. How incredible that I should be saying such things—I who had never dared a word of disrespect!

But why didn't he call? What was he waiting for? Was he waiting for me to say my worst so as to be able to whip me all the harder? The rain drizzled down. The day was gray and quiet. The whole thing began to seem unreal. The absence of reaction was as incredible as the defamation. Both seemed impossible. It was a bleak and sinister dream.

But it's real! I thought furiously. I *had* said those things, and would keep on saying them till I made him answer. I became frantic, poured out a tirade of abuse, searched my memory for every dirty word I knew, and when the store of profanity was exhausted and I stopped, breathless, to listen . . . there was no response.

"You goddamn dirty son of a bitch!" I screamed, "I wish you was dead! I wish you was dead, do you hear? Do you hear me?"

I had finished. Now something would happen. I cowered and waited for it, but there was no word from the porch. Not a sound. Not even the stir of bedclothes.

The rage passed and I became miserable. I sat with arms around my knees, staring blankly at the indifferent rain. As the minutes went by, I became more appalled by what I had done. Its meaning broadened, expanded in endless ramifications, became boundless and unforgivable. I had broken the commandment to honor thy father and mother. I had taken the name of the Lord in vain, and that was the same as cursing God. I thought of my mother. What would she say when she learned? I pictured her face. She would cry.

For another half hour I sat there. I no longer expected to be called. For some reason the matter was to be left in abeyance. Finally, unable to endure further waiting, I got up and walked away. I went to the barn and wandered about morosely, expecting momentarily to see my mother enter to say that my father wanted me, but she did not come, and the morning passed without further incident.

On entering the house for dinner, my first concern was to learn whether she knew. When she smiled, I knew that she did not. Now that I was indoors I knew something would happen. I stayed as far from the porch as possible and spoke in low tones. Yet my father must know me to be present. I could not eat, and soon left the house and went back to the barn, where I felt somewhat less vulnerable.

I spent the afternoon there alone, sitting on a box, waiting. Occasionally I would get up and walk around aimlessly. Sometimes I would stand in the doorway looking out at the rain. Unrestrained, I felt myself a prisoner. I searched through my small understanding of my father but found no explanation of the delay. It was unlike him to postpone a whipping. Then it occurred to me that what I had done might so far have exceeded ordinary transgression as to require a special punishment. Perhaps I would not be whipped at all but sent away from home, never be permitted to come back.

When suppertime came, I sneaked into the house, tried to be inconspicuous, but was so agitated that my mother was concerned. She looked at me inquiringly, ran her hand affectionately through my hair. "What's the matter, son? Don't you feel well? You look all worn out."

"I feel all right," I said.

I escaped her and sat alone on the back porch until called to the table. When supper was safely over, my situation was unimproved. It was too late to go outside again, and I could not long remain in the house without meeting my father. At the latest it could be put off only till family prayer. Perhaps that was the time when my crime would be related. Maybe they would pray for me and then expel me from home. I had just begun drying the dishes when the long-awaited sound was heard.

"Son."

It was not the wrathful voice I had expected. It was calm, just loud enough to be heard, but enough to make me tremble and drop a spoon. For a moment it seemed I could not move.

"Your daddy wants you, dear."

I put down the dishtowel and went to the door of the porch. "Yes, sir."

"Come out here where I can see you."

I approached the bed. My hands were clenched and I was biting my lip, trying not to cry.

"Your mother tells me you haven't been eating well today. You aren't sick, are you?"

"No, sir."

"You feel all right?"

"Yes, sir."

"Sit down, son. I called you out here to talk a while. I often think we don't talk to each other enough. I guess that's my fault. We'll have to do better in the future. I'd like to hear more about what you're interested in and what you think, because that's the only way I can get to know you." He paused a moment. "Maybe you think because I'm grown-up, I understand everything, but that's not true. You'll find as you get older that no matter how much you learn, there's always much you don't know. For example, you're my own son and I ought to know you pretty well, but every now and then something'll happen that'll make me realize I don't understand you at all."

I choked back a sob, braced myself for the coming blow.

"I don't think I ever understood my own father," he went on presently, "until it was too late. We were very poor—much poorer, son, than you can imagine. From year in to year out we might see only a few dollars in our house, and what little there was had to be saved for essentials. When we sold our cotton, we'd have to buy a plow or an ax. And there were staple foods we had to buy like flour and sugar. We bought cloth, too, but never any ready-made clothes. Until I was a grown man I never had any clothes except what my mother made. I got my first store-bought suit to go away to medical school in, and I don't believe my mother ever had a store-bought dress. My father worked hard and made his boys work hard. We resented it and sometimes even hated him for it, but in the end we knew he was right. One of my brothers never could get along with Daddy, and he ran away from home when he was fifteen. He turned out to be a no-account scoundrel, and the last I heard of him he was a saloon keeper in New Orleans.

"In the summer we hoed corn and picked cotton, and in the winter we fixed rail fences and chopped wood and hauled it home. And always there were mules and pigs to take care of.

It was a very different life from yours . . . and in some ways a better one." He looked at me affectionately. "At any rate, we learned how to work, and there's nothing more important for a boy to learn. It's something you haven't yet learned, son. Isn't that right?"

"Yes, sir."

"You will, though. If you ever amount to anything, you'll learn. You're learning now. I wish you could understand, though, that I wouldn't be trying to teach you so fast if I knew I would live long enough to teach you more slowly." He paused. "Do you have anything to say?"

"No, sir."

"Then I guess you'd better see if your mother needs you."

I stood up, hardly able to believe that this was all.

"Son."

"Yes, sir."

"Come here a minute."

I went to the bed and my father put a hand on my shoulder. "Remember, son," he said in a husky voice, "whenever it seems I'm being hard on you . . . it's because I love you."

LATE THAT NIGHT I woke in terror from a nightmare. For several minutes I lay in bed trembling, unable to convince myself that it was just a dream. Presently I got up and tiptoed through the dark house to the porch.

"Daddy?" I whispered. "Daddy . . . are you all right?"

There was no reply, but soon I became aware of his regular breathing. I went back to bed but almost immediately got up and knelt on the floor. "Dear God, please don't let anything happen to Daddy. Amen."

Still I could not sleep. I lay in bed and thought of many things and after a while began worrying about the razor. What had I done with it? Was it still on the ground under the awning? Perhaps I had left it open. Someone might step on it and get cut. I got up again and went outside looking for it. In the dark I felt about on the ground under my father's windows but did not find it. Then I went to the barn and found it in its usual place, properly closed.

The next morning before noon, I finished the job. The last blade of grass was cut and carried away and the backyard was as bald as a razor could make it.

"Daddy," I said, standing under the porch windows, "I've finished. Is it all right?"

He looked over the yard, then took his binoculars and scrutinized it in more detail, particularly the corners.

"That's well done, son."

I put away the basket and razor and came inside. After dinner I began to feel uncomfortable. It seemed strange not to be working. Restless, unable to sit still, I wandered about the house, looking out the windows, wondering what to do. Presently I sought and obtained permission to go to Paul's house, but somehow felt I was doing something wrong.

During the next two weeks I often played with my friends but never fully lost myself in play and was secretly glad when school started and life settled down to a routine again. I was more quiet than before and better behaved, and when next the report cards were distributed I had a nearly perfect score in conduct.

ONCE A WEEK an iron pot hangs from a tripod over a wood fire. My father watches from the house. When the water comes to a boil, my mother puts in the sheets, tells me to stir, and I poke at them with a broom handle, driving them down, and they gurgle and foam and surge upward, ever more violently, steam rising, swaying, swirling around me, the fire getting hotter, my face burning, sweat dripping. My mother then removes the sheets with the broom handle, throws them over the clothesline, empties the pot, removes the tripod. "Go inside now," she says.

From the house my father and I watch as she spreads the fire and then, one by one, carefully, places the accumulated sputum cups in the bed of red coals.

"I like to see them burn," my father says.

Sometimes three or four, sometimes seven or eight, white waxed cardboard boxes, each filled with thick mucus, yellow and green and red—my father's inner substance—lined up one after another in the seething fire, a train of little coffins describing my father's downhill slide through the week.

"Millions of tubercle bacilli," my father says. "Maybe billions. They're eating my lungs out. They are going to kill me."

Suddenly he cries out: "The sputum is putting out the fire! Build it up, son! Pile on more wood!"

I rush outside. "Keep away!" my mother says.

"But Daddy . . . "

"Stand back!" she says abruptly. "These things explode, splatter germs."

She herself adds the wood, while I go back inside. I am in thrall to my father's despair. From the window he watches with a manic stare. "Out there," he murmurs, "I can destroy them. But in here"—he taps his chest, presently turns on me accusingly—"If I could just *get inside*, in here"—he taps his chest more urgently—"and scratch out the cavities, clean them out with a knife . . . then paint the walls with iodine. . . ."

I have the sense of being addressed, not as a child, not as a son, but as a mysterious stranger. I am being made to bear witness to his case against God.

A PAROXYSM OF coughing throws him forward, half upright in bed, rocks him back and forth, side to side. He grabs the sputum cup, holds it to his mouth. Blood and purulent mucus gush forth. He supports himself on his left elbow as, gradually, the spell subsides. He replaces the cup on the bedside table, lifts the covers, looks down the length of his body—gaunt, heaving rib cage, sunken belly, stick legs, and, springing up from this wasteland, obelisk in the desert, a gigantic erection. He sees me looking from the doorway, drops the covers. I watch the somber eyes look me over, take me into account: those eyes, I think, are meditating that I will live while he will die. "Go back to your work, son."

In the evening when the chores are done, my mother sits with him, mending clothes. The light fails, the summer evening turns to dusk, to night. He is very weak, does not move, can hardly speak. She lays aside her sewing, turns on the light, stands beside the bed, looks down at him, takes his hand. He looks up at her in pain and foreboding. She is frightened, tries to control it, to deny it. She sits again, rocks slightly. She is terrified of losing him, of being alone.

A still night, not a breath of air. The faint hum of insects. A deep silence. Suddenly a violent flurry of feathers. She starts, jumps up. Gray wings are beating on the screen wire. Claws and tawny beadlike eyes appear for a moment. Then nothing. Then deep silence again. She turns to him. A messenger, she thinks, then denies it: "It's so sultry . . . there'll be a storm."

Again she moves to the bed, stands beside him. He turns aside his head. "Look at me," she says. "Can I do something for you?" Slowly he moves his head side to side. "I want you to feel better. I want you to get strong again."

He looks up at her from a deep hole. She is a reed, will fall to the first man who lays hands on her. "I would feel better," he whispers, "if I knew . . . that you . . . would not marry again."

She is astonished: "I want you to get *well!*"

He brushes this aside. "Promise me: When I die . . . you will not . . . marry again." His bony fingers sink into her flesh. "I promise," she says.

AS MY FATHER sank into darkness my world filled with light.

Before sunrise, someone tugging at my sleeve. "Wake up!

Wake up!" my sister whispers. "Daddy's real sick." Shadowy figures, edged in lamplight, hover about the bed. Dr. Whittaker leans forward, motionless, stethoscope to my father's chest. Behind him, leaning forward in the same curve of frozen apprehension, my mother seems to hold her breath. Minutes pass. Nothing happens. Nothing, I think, will happen. My father is often "real sick."

Now I make out the figures of Mr. and Mrs. Means in the shadows, motionless, listening. My sister stands in the doorway. The room becomes strangely purple. I look from one to another of the still, waiting faces. A slight tint of pink touches these faces, then a wave of light washes up around us. I turn, catch the first rim of sun slicing up through the horizon, into the pale green sky. The air around us becomes more strongly pink. Still nothing happens.

Then, suddenly, a horizontal beam of golden light flashes across the room, splatters on the porcelain music box, splinters on the stethoscope, the clock, becomes incandescent in my mother's dark hair. Dr. Whittaker slowly straightens up, folds the stethoscope, turns. My mother, mouth open, eyes wide with agony, strains against what's coming. "He's gone." She flinches as if to a whip, a shudder sweeps across her body, she reels back uttering a scream so loud, so hoarse, of such deep pain, the scream of a large animal that has been struck a mortal blow—a scream that tears through me like a spear, that I hear still in the roots of my teeth. *Who/what is she crying for? Regret over the intimacy never had?*

A FEW DAYS later, at noon, the brilliant light falling vertically in golden shafts, and all around us the intense green of the grass, the red and yellow of roses set in vases before the gray stones, the purple of peonies and pink oleander, and above us the light green of the leaves, and overall the clear blue sky. Amidst all this color we make our way, about thirty of us, through the cemetery.

My mother walks slowly, I on one side holding her hand, my sister on the other. We seat ourselves in the first row of folding chairs. Directly before us is a trestle of steel on which black-suited men now place the coffin. People arrive slowly, seating themselves behind us, the minister taking a stand to one side, the funeral director folding back the upper half of the coffin lid. My father is clad in a navy blue suit, white shirt, dark tie. A stranger. I have trouble recognizing him, knew him only in the gray pajamas of illness. The eyes that have seen through me all these years are closed, the face that relentlessly condemned my flawed and wayward character is waxen and still— pointed upward, almost as if straining upward, to escape the coffin, dignified but helpless, the long thin nose like the keel of an upturned ship.

Beneath the steel trestle is a green cloth simulating grass. It is sagging, thereby revealing the grave it is meant to deny. Two black-suited men stretch it taut. The minister places a hymn book on the music stand, raises his arms. "Brethren . . . let us harken to the words of our Saviour Jesus Christ."

Directly behind the coffin is something standing up vertically, about five feet high, covered with a green felt cloth. I turn to my aunt Mit on my left, whisper, "What is that?" and point. "Shhhh," she says.

" 'Let not your heart be troubled,' " the minister intones, " 'ye believe in God, believe also in me.' " I turn to my mother, touch her arm. Her lips are moving. The minister continues: " 'In my Father's house are many mansions: if it were not so, I would have told you. I go to prepare a place for you. And if I go and prepare a place for you, I will come again, and receive you unto myself; that where I am, there ye may be also. And whither I go ye know, and the way ye know.' "

"Mama," I whisper, "Mama, is that thing . . . a piano?" I point at the green mound.

"Shhhh," she whispers. Her eyes are red, tears run down

her face, dropping in her lap. In the brilliant light I see the fine hair at the line of her chin, the tear detained in that hair. The glare makes me squint. The sun is beating on the blue sky as on a drum. The heat falls in waves. I itch and squirm in my wool jacket.

At a gesture we stand. The minister closes his eyes, recites a prayer, raising his voice as if to loft the prayer heavenward.

It *is* a piano, I decide. It is exactly the shape of the upright piano in our church, and is covered by the same green felt. That slight bulge about the middle is the keyboard. Presently, the minister will pull off the cover and someone will play. Maybe my mother will play. When they lower the body into the grave . . . that's when . . . *then* she will play. Maybe "After the Ball Is Over" or "The Burning of Rome." Another prayer. Then we are asked to stand to sing a hymn. *Now*, I think, now they will take off the cover. The hymn is finished. We sit again. Then another prayer.

And then, suddenly, it is over. My mother is approaching the coffin, leading me by the hand. Someone holds out to her a paper bag of rose petals. She takes a few, drops them on the coffin. We move on. Looking back, I see others doing the same, one after another, putting their hands in the bag, taking out the rose petals, dropping them on the coffin. Now we are walking down the path. "Isn't anybody going to play the piano?" I ask, and my mother bursts into sobs. In the limousine I try once more. "Mama, what was that green thing? What was under that green cloth? Was it a piano?"

"No." Her eyes are dry and bleak, look over me to a desolate future. "It was . . . dirt . . . to fill the grave."

III

GOOD-BYE, MAMA

DOWNTOWN SAN ANTONIO. An old man with a pushcart. Dilapidated felt hat, deeply creased with a spreading sweat stain, blue shirt, baggy pants, scraggly salt-and-pepper beard, red nose, pale twinkling eyes under bushy gray eyebrows, a wizened smile and a wink for my mother. Before him a small chopping board, a sizzling grill, buns and pretzels in the glass warming oven. My mother is pondering whether she can afford to buy me a treat.

Seeing us watching, he takes a sausage in his left hand, holds it aloft. Plump as if to burst, thick as a man's arm, red and shining. He lowers it to the board and draws across it a long, heavy knife, first in the air as if to savor the cut; then, lowering the edge, he pulls the knife slowly toward himself, hunching his shoulders and sucking in his breath, as a slice of sausage peels away. A lascivious moment, a shudder of relaxation. He impales the slice of sausage on the knife, advances it toward me as if to drop it in my hands, or perhaps to impale me too, all with a droll expression on his mischievous face, then, smoothly rotating his body, drops it on the smoking grill, where it sizzles with the spicy aroma of pepper and pork and frying fat.

Amid a flutter of wings, a pigeon alights on the cart. With a snakelike sweep of his left hand, the old man scoops up the bird, forces the legs into extension, lowers it to the chopping board. Glancing at me with that mischievous grin, he whacks off the pigeon's feet. With his left hand he throws aloft the shocked bird as, with his right, holding the knife, he brushes to the ground the twitching feet.

My mother utters an anguished cry, clutches me to her, trembles, pulls me away.

AT NINE, I passionately wanted a certain type of scooter. Two wheels in back, one in front, a platform to stand on that tilted forward and back with the shift in one's weight, this movement being translated by gears into the rotation of the rear wheels. My mother and sister and I were living on eighty dollars a month; and this scooter, my mother told me, was beyond our means. But I would not give up. I begged, I pleaded, I suggested that we could do without certain other things deemed to be necessities. I made budgets. We didn't have to get it right now, I said, it could be for Christmas. She was going to spend *something* for Christmas, anyway. "Please, Mama, don't say no, say at least maybe." So finally, to get some peace, she said, "Well, maybe," and of course that meant yes. So then I pestered her to buy it soon, buy it now, "Please, Mama, because if you wait till December they will all be sold." But she does not have the money now. She could make a deposit, I tell her. Just so they'll hold it. And again, finally, she says, "Well, maybe," which means yes.

But now I wonder: Has she actually done it? She tends to procrastinate. Maybe she's putting it off. So I start in on her about that. Has she actually, *really*, made the deposit? "I can't say," she says. "It's supposed to be for Christmas—isn't it?— if you get it? It's supposed to be a *surprise*." But I want to *know*. I want to be sure. "You don't have to *tell* me," I say to her. "You don't have to say *anything* in words. I'll just ask you, 'Have you already got it?' and *if* you've got it, just move your eyelids a little bit."

She looks at me wonderingly. She is sitting on the back steps of our little house, I standing before her, bare feet in the still-warm earth. Dusk. Around us the empty flatness of Texas. The pink glow of sunset beginning to go purple. She leans forward, elbows on her knees. A pretty woman, still young, alone, poor, insecure, two children . . . and I before her, twisting her fingers. *"Please, Mama!"* She gazes at me, her hands inert in my entreating and manipulative grasp. She looks away at the darkening horizon. I wait. And then, slowly, her eyelids flicker.

I LIE ON my cot on the back porch, sleepless. A summer night. I am drenched in silver light. Silence, stillness. Not a leaf moves. Yet high above there must be a wind, for dark clouds move slowly across the full moon. The air is warm, humid, a smell of honeysuckle. Tornado weather. I push down the covers. The moon gleams its radiant invitation. I sleep briefly, wake with a start. The moon has disappeared. I feel an ache, a distant agitation.

I make my way through the dark house to my mother's room. "Mama." She moves, wakes. "What? What is it?" "I can't sleep, Mama. Can I come in with you?" "Of course you can." She lifts the covers. I climb in beside her, facing the window. She spoons herself behind me, enfolds me in her arms, her heat. I feel comforted, sleepy. The moon was drawing me out-side, into the night; now what is inside, the two of us together, the warmth of our bodies, has become more weighty; the darkening and brightening moon is far away.

How long have I slept? My mother, behind me, has turned away, is snoring. Before me the open window, the warm, scented air drifting over us. The chinaberry tree, the mesquite, the honeysuckle, all are dripping molten silver. The silence is vast and heavy, hangs like ripe fruit. I roll over on my left side, lie against my mother's back. Her nightgown has ridden up about her waist; I feel the warmth, the firmness, the mass and curves of her buttocks. I put my arm across her, my hand coming to rest on her belly. My throat constricts. The fingers venture lower, encounter the crinkly hair. I am motionless, breathe slowly, deeply, through my mouth: If she wakes she must find me asleep, must assume it by chance that my hand has found its way to this place. But she is undisturbed, her gentle snoring regular.

After a while my fingers begin their prowl. I seek an entrance. The skin from which this hair springs is firm, mounded, spongy. Where is it? I move slowly from side to side, from top to bottom, find nothing. An impenetrable wall. I am shut out. Yet it *must* be here . . . somewhere. A choked feeling in my throat, a strangled acrid taste. I wait a while, try again, feel my way back and forth through every smallest part of this baffling triangle.

The snoring stops. I lie as if frozen. Minutes pass . . . an eternity . . . the two of us motionless in an impenetrably dense silence. Neither of us breathes. I should snore to let her know that I am asleep, but am paralyzed. After a while she sighs, extends her legs a bit, shifts her position. My inert hand is still in her tangle of hair. We have come uncovered in this warm night. Minutes pass. Her breathing becomes deep, she resumes her gentle snoring. I relax. Behind my back the silver light comes and goes as the high clouds pass before the moon, and directly before me the moon of her behind gleams and disappears, gleams, winks, disappears.

She rolls over on her back. Under cover of her sleep, I resume my stealthy search. Her legs have fallen somewhat apart—an opportunity lost to me because my only map for this primal quest is the drawings of naked women on toilet walls, which portray an oval orifice fringed with hair in the lower abdominal wall. In that mysterious triangle back and forth my fingers go. An unbroken barrier. *It's not here!* My assault on a walled city is repulsed without even rousing the sleeping defenders. I withdraw my hand, impotent, humiliated, roll over on my right side facing the window. The moon regards me with an ironic stare, comes and goes with the dark clouds: "Here I am, now I'm gone! Catch me if you can!" A sour taste of defeat, of weakness, of rancor. I leave her, return to my cot on the back porch.

The next morning, getting dressed, hearing her move about in the kitchen, preparing breakfast, I think: If she is disapproving, she was awake; if not, she was asleep. As it turns out, she is unusually tender and loving with me throughout the day. But I am surly.

AT ELEVEN, I discover chess. Mr. Allison, a deacon of the church, shows me the moves. I am enthralled. Dazzling possibilities beckon. There before me, on that board, the most ruthless power, with murder in view, may be pursued, lawfully, permissibly, through patterns of great beauty, of intricate intellectuality. An immaculate sublimation, a red carpet for warded-off aggression. I ransack the chess shelf in the public library, study openings, mid-games, end games, begin to go for a Morphy-style, open game of reckless, slashing advance; and if, by profligate sacrifice, I can bring it about that only on my last breath, with my last ounce of strength, do I drive a dagger through the heart of the enemy king, then so much more grand the victory.

A few weeks later, in the evening, I am again in Mr.

Allison's home, facing him over a board. Mrs. Allison sits nearby, knitting, rocking gently in her chair. Their children are grown and married; the two of them live alone in a small house at the end of a dirt road. He is a carpenter, a devout man; she teaches Sunday School.

I move rapidly. Mr. Allison, shaken by my precocious mastery, takes his time, proceeds warily. Two hours go by. I feel the need to urinate. Gradually I am closing in, forcing him into a losing position. I advance a rook to the seventh rank. The pressure on his castled king is mounting, as is also the pressure in my bladder. Where is the bathroom? I look about surreptitiously. A tiny house, flimsy walls. They would hear the stream. Mrs. Allison knits calmly. The room is deathly silent. Mr. Allison moves a rook to the open queen's rook's file. His attack is coming too late, I've already got my teeth in his throat. An exchange of bishops enables me to put a knight on king knight 5. I squirm on the plush couch, rock slowly, front to back, side to side. Mrs. Allison rocks placidly in her chair. Why don't I ask? The overwhelming humiliation of the question . . . the intrusion of bodily need . . . I can't. I writhe. Why doesn't he move? Why doesn't he resign? Can't he *see* it's hopeless? Why don't *I* resign? . . . But with a sure win . . . it's crazy, would be perverse. If I should ask to use the bathroom, they would *hear*. Mr. Allison ponders patiently. I make little hopping movements. It shakes the table. He adjusts the pieces. The pain is unbearable.

Then it happens. Exploding. Suddenly, copiously, irresistibly flowing, silently, down my leg, into my shoe, onto the floor. With slow inevitability the smell of warm urine and wet wool rises between us. Mr. Allison shifts slightly, but—God rest his soul!— says not a word, registers the mishap only by taking somewhat less time with his next several moves and soon resigning.

I disappear into the night, in my wet pants and squishy shoe, know that I can never enter that house again.

WHEN I WAS fourteen, my sister went away to college. My mother and I were now alone with each other. In the mornings she would get up first and prepare breakfast, which we would then eat together. She would leave for work the same time I left for school. She taught third grade, and I was a junior in high school. When we arrived back home in the afternoons she would often walk the mile or so to the grocery store. Returning, she would make beds, sweep, clean, wash, and prepare dinner. Afterward she would wash the dishes while I studied. When all the chores were done she would sit at the kitchen table with checkbook, budget, bills all spread out before her and "do the accounts," as she put it, which meant trying to figure out whether we could make it to the end of the month, and if not what expenses could be cut, or postponed. She had "no head for figures," as she said, so this was a tedious and inconclusive task, always to be continued the next night. Sitting at the table under the dim hanging light, she pondered, she moved her lips, repeatedly moistened the pencil on her tongue as if a hyperreadiness to write might make the bleak figures come out better, a deeply troubled expression on her face. If I showed concern, she reassured me. "Oh, don't worry, son. We will find a way." Or, "It will all turn out for the best. God will look after us." But she didn't act as if she counted on help, from any source, but as if it were all up to her and she were failing.

About this time I gained a different image of her, came to see her life not simply as she lived it day to day, but in extension. For six years she had enslaved herself to my father, a twenty-four-hour nursing duty, day after day. And the outcome of all those years of toil and devotion: he died, he was gone, and that wild piercing cry she flung after him, and no response, nothing. Where he had been was but a void.

She pulled herself together then, but only to begin a different kind of servitude: to her children. She had no special training or ability or experience, and no confidence in herself. She offered piano lessons, sold encyclopedias, finally got a job as study hall teacher, went to night school and summer school, eventually obtained a temporary teacher's certificate that had to be renewed each year by more courses. She was never sure we could make it. She knew we would not starve, for, at worst, we could move back to Louisiana and live with her parents and brothers; but it seemed important to her, for her children, that we have a home of our own. This was what she was struggling to achieve and to maintain. And was succeeding—but just barely.

It was then I came to see where her life was heading, and that she herself could neither see what lay ahead nor do anything about it: She enslaved herself to those who would leave her. June had already gone, and in two years I would be leaving—I could hardly wait. Then she would be alone. I worried about what would happen after I left.

I began to help her in ways she would never have thought to ask. I took the list from her hand in the afternoons and walked to the store and came back with the groceries. I helped as she cooked our dinner. We washed the dishes together. I urged her to go out socially, to meet people. She was forty and I told her she should get married. She gratefully accepted my greater participation, and listened to my counsel with a kind of hungry bemusement. It meant a lot to her that I was talking to her, that I was urging something on her, that I was concerned, but the content of my urgings passed her by. I told her of specific social opportunities—a church picnic, a group of schoolteachers who met for square dancing, excursions to the Spanish missions. It was too late; these things seemed remote to her. What was real was that I needed new shoes and June needed an evening dress—and where would she find the money to send me to college? Where there should have been concern for self was concern only for us.

Two more years pass, and now I am sixteen and she is forty-two. I have graduated from high school, and, as she feared, there is no money to send me to college. So she writes to her brother, O.M., in Baton Rouge; and O.M. invites me to live with him and to attend Louisiana State University.

Now she is alone. She writes almost every day, and her letters are dull, dull, dull; for there's not much of interest to be extracted from her cramped routine. And I write to her several times each week because I don't want her to be disappointed. I know the pattern of her days, see her getting home about four in the afternoon after a long walk from school, tired and dusty, hasn't eaten, yet before entering the house she crosses the road to the row of mailboxes, and I feel how she will feel if the box is empty. And my letters to her are dull, dull, dull; for there's not much of interest to be extracted from dutifulness and guilt.

At Christmas I am home. She looks tired, thin. I ask about her eating. She brushes me aside. I persist and discover that she cooks very little. Mostly she eats scraps, whatever is at hand, often forgets. I scold her and lecture her; she thrives on my concern and promises to change. The spring semester passes, and I am again home for the summer. June graduates from college and gets a teaching job in Port Arthur, and in September I return to Baton Rouge.

Two weeks later my mother mentions being sick, has missed two days of school, but says she is already better. Her sister is coming to visit. Then nothing. I hear next from her sister, my aunt Mit, who writes that she found my mother so weak she could not bear to leave her alone in San Antonio and so took her back with her to Comfort, Texas, where Mit's husband, Ike, is telegrapher on a spur line of the Southern Pacific. I continue to write encouragement and advice and continue to receive nondescript letters of vague optimism. In every letter she is "beginning to feel better." Then comes a letter from Mit saying that my mother is much worse; Mit is worried about having her there where no doctor is available, yet believes my mother to be too sick to be at home alone. Mit can't go with her to San Antonio and stay with her, because she has a husband and two children of her own to look after.

I leave Baton Rouge the next day, changing in San Antonio to the freight train to Comfort, traveling in the caboose, which I have all to myself—except occasionally when the conductor climbs down from the roof to sit by the round coal-burning stove. The conductor lets me off at the switching station near Comfort.

The tiny three-room house where my aunt and uncle live is no more than six feet from the tracks, yellow clapboard like all the company buildings along the Southern Pacific line. On the other side of the tracks is the tiny room where my uncle works as telegrapher.

I enter the house. No one expects me. My aunt, astonished, takes me to my mother's room. I open the door, see her lying in bed, propped up on pillows. Her face is gaunt, the skin ashen, her white hair splayed out on the pillow, her eyes large and frightened. I see the shock of surprise sweep over her face, followed by a wave of doubt—she fears she is hallucinating— her mouth opens; the face contorts in anguish, hope, and disbelief.

"It's me, Mama. I've come to take you home."

In San Antonio I take her to see Dr. Whittaker, who never charged us, and who now listens to her tale. She is nervous, her hands tremble, her limbs are weak, her gait unsteady, she has no appetite, has frequent hot flashes, and a peculiar rash on her arms and legs. Pellagra, he says, and prescribes a diet high in vitamin B with many leafy vegetables. She is too weak to be up, so I am the cook, and now do for her as she did for my father. I prepare the food, serve it to her in bed on a tray, urge her to eat, to force it down if necessary; and she does.

And then begins a diarrhea that eventually becomes bloody. Dr. Whittaker now puts her on a cereal diet; I prepare the brown mush three times a day. The diarrhea continues, the nervousness gets worse. Dr. Whittaker begins talking about a "hidden focus of infection," and goes looking: bladder, kidneys, tonsils. Finds nothing. He tries a drug for amoebic dysentery—just in case, he says. Nothing helps.

Weeks pass, months. Winter with its rains. She cries a lot, she trembles, she can't stand without support. Every few weeks we go back to see Dr. Whittaker. He is at a loss, is casting about.

"There *must* be a hidden focus of infection," he says. And since everything else, he thinks, has been excluded, "It must be the teeth."

"My teeth don't hurt," my mother says. "That's maybe the one thing that seems all right."

"Nevertheless, it must be the teeth," he says. "To be safe, I think we'd better have them out."

"All of them?"

"Yes."

My mother is shocked. At home she feels her teeth one by one with her fingers, tries to wiggle them; they are firm. "What should I do?" she cries. I do not know. I examine them myself. Her teeth are white and regular, I can't see anything wrong with them, but it has been explained to us that the infection may be at the roots and may not show. The only thing certain is that she is very sick and not getting better. We have no money with which to seek a second opinion, we do not know that this is urgently indicated, nor would we know where to seek it. "I don't know, Mama. I just don't know." We go to see Dr. Whittaker again: "In my opinion, Mrs. Wheelis, you should have these teeth removed." Her lips tremble; her forefinger resting on her worn purse makes frantic little waving movements. She acquiesces.

Now begins the grisly ordeal, four teeth a week. All are difficult extractions, usually with broken bone and broken roots. Each Friday morning we plod to the trolley, ride into the city. She emerges from the dentist's office, holding a bloody towel to her mouth. She can't speak. I comfort her on the trolley, tell her that though this is very hard and difficult now, maybe in time it will make her well. At the end of the line we get off; the motorman looks at us curiously. I hold her arm and support her around the waist as we slowly make our way on foot the mile to our house. She can't speak, is in an anguish of pain, of dismay at what is happening to her. In eight weeks all thirty-two teeth are removed. She is forty-four years old.

Now we must wait for healing before dentures can be fitted. I feed her liquids and puréed vegetables. Gradually she begins to feel better. We believe that the hidden focus of infection has been removed, that now perhaps she will recover. The diarrhea is not so bad, she can walk. She has gained some strength. An impression is made for her dentures. She begins to look forward to being able to chew again, to eat solid food.

Eventually the great day arrives: we are to pick up the dentures at noon. I buy a steak, plan a celebratory meal, promise her a treat.

She looks puzzled as she emerges from the dentist's office. "Let me see," I say. She shakes her head. On the trolley she doesn't want to talk. "They feel strange," she says finally. "Let me see." She opens her mouth slightly. "They look fine," I tell her. She is nervous, unhappy. At home she lies on the bed, fans herself, is having hot flashes. I set the table, cut flowers in the yard, grill the steak. The festive meal is ready. She comes to the table. Her hands tremble. I watch as she cuts the meat, lifts a small piece to her mouth. A tentative effort to chew, instantly aborted. Her face is still. The eyes fill with tears. She removes the meat from her mouth, begins to weep.

"I can't eat!" she wails. She rises from the table, flings herself through the house, onto the bed. I follow.

"It just takes time, Mama. You have to be patient. It will get better."

She sobs inconsolably.

ALL OF HER symptoms now get worse again: weakness, diarrhea, nervousness, hot flashes. The rash, however, has disappeared.

One night I wake to find her standing by my cot. "Son!"

"What is it, Mama?"

She trembles. "I'm frightened."

"What are you afraid of?"

"I don't know."

"Did you have a bad dream?"

"No. I can't sleep." She shifts back and forth, one foot to the other. "Come lie with me for a while, son. Maybe that will help me."

I sit up on my cot, switch on the hanging light. She is shaking slightly, twisting her hands. I get up, put my arm around her. "Come on, Mama. I'll stay with you." I take her back to her room. She crawls into bed, holds open the covers for me. I sit on the edge of the bed, observe her disappointment. Again she holds up the covers for me to enter, desperate entreaty on her face. I think of all those times when *I* was frightened and was made welcome to come into this bed. And I remember, too, that night when I was *not* frightened, but still was welcome, the night of the mysterious moon and the sailing clouds.

"I will do just about anything for you, Mama. But you mustn't ask me to come to bed with you." She lets the covers fall. "But I'll help you go to sleep." I turn off the light. "You're in your own bed now, and I'm right here beside you . . . looking after you . . . and nothing bad is going to happen. I'm going to stay right here with you. You've been hard sick . . . have gone through a bad time . . . but the worst is over and now you are beginning to get better." My tone is heavy, prophetic, incantatory. "Close your eyes now . . . because it is time for you to sleep. I'm going to stay right here with you. And I will tell you a story . . . and when I finish, you will be asleep. And while you listen, I want you to imagine something very heavy, a heavy stone perhaps. It is in your hands. Right now. You feel its heaviness . . . now. It's in your eyelids, too. And I am telling you a story . . . about something that happened a long time ago . . . about a man who carried a stone just like the one in your hands and felt all of its great heaviness . . . the same heaviness you feel now in your eyelids. . . ."

GRADUALLY SHE IMPROVED. After a year she was able to be up and about. Her strength came back, but not completely. The illness had diminished her, left her weaker, more vulnerable. She was forty-five. Her hair was snow white, her hands trembled, her eyes were very blue. She was well enough, I thought, for me to leave her, but not well enough for me to leave her alone. With difficulty I persuade her to put our house in the hands of a real estate agent and go back to Louisiana to live with her parents.

THE TWO OF us sit on a bench in the waiting room of the railroad station in San Antonio. My mother is wearing a black dress, shapeless and old. I sense in her a mounting agitation, and in myself a corresponding fear; I try to escape from both by pretending to read. The book in my hands is Kant's *Critique of Pure Reason*. She tries not to break in upon my apparent absorption.

At last, unable to keep still any longer, she asks, "What did we do with the living-room set?"

"Left it in the house," I murmur, without looking up from my book.

"Left it in the house?"

"You know that, Mother. We discussed it often enough," I say patiently.

"We shouldn't have left it," she says. "That's not the right kind of furniture to leave in a rented house. It's solid walnut. Your daddy bought it for me at an auction. We should have put it in storage."

The station vibrates slightly to an arriving train. I look at the clock and then across the waiting room to the bulletin board, where the incoming and outgoing trains are indicated in white chalk. There is still half an hour before the departure time of our trains, due to leave at almost the same moment, for different destinations. I try to go on reading, find that I can't concentrate, and close the book. My glance comes to rest first on my own luggage, a single suitcase, and then on my mother's four suitcases, two of them shabby and dilapidated, with heavy cord tied around them to keep them from bursting open.

"Don't you want me to check those two old suitcases?" I ask.

She does not appear to hear me. Her lips move, as if she is talking to herself.

"Mother," I say, touching her arm and then indicating the dilapidated suitcases. "I'd better check those two on your ticket."

"What's that?" she cries, her voice full of alarm. "What are you going to do?"

"I'm going to check your bags," I say, and stand up.

"No," she says. "Don't do that."

"You can't manage four by yourself," I say. "You have to change at Shreveport and Monroe. What if you can't find a redcap?"

"Hon," she says, brushing this problem aside, "where did we put that little baby dress of yours?"

I sigh and sit down. "I don't know. But it doesn't matter. It was falling apart anyway."

"Why, dear! I wouldn't part with that dress for the world. It's pure silk. Your grandmother spent months making it—before you were born. Didn't you see the fine handwork on it?"

"Yes," I say wearily. "I saw it. Don't worry. It must be in one of the boxes we stored. It's bound to be there, because we didn't throw anything away. Nothing. Not even a thirty-year-old newspaper."

"I wish I could remember where my things are," she says plaintively.

Nervous and withdrawn, she sits and clutches her purse. A gray-haired Negro, red cap in hand, plants himself in front of the bulletin board and in a long, rolling cadence announces the arrival and impending departure of the *Sunset Limited*. Suddenly, Mama leans forward and unties the cord around one of the old suitcases. In spite of my protests, she opens the suitcase and begins going through the contents.

The bag is filled with fragments of the past, carefully folded and lovingly packed: surgical instruments that had belonged to my father; a souvenir of Lookout Mountain; a wedding veil; baby shoes; a bullet mold that was used by my great-grandfather; sheet music; bundles of ancient letters; a certificate of membership in the Woodmen of the World, dated 1905.

Many of these things I had previously thrown away as being of no value, and the rest I had put away for storage. She must have been up most of the preceding night retrieving and packing them.

Since she could never throw anything away, the closets and the attic had been piled high with old possessions, and the process of sorting and packing had brought to light innumerable items evocative of the past. Though ostensibly engaged in discarding the useless and packing the valuable, actually she had done neither. She had merely gone through our belongings one by one, fondled them, talked about them, and cried now and then. At the end of a morning's work, she would be surrounded by piles of souvenirs, from not one of which was she willing to be separated.

I, on the other hand, had ransacked ruthlessly, and my mother had spent much of her time recovering the things I had thrown away. The work of one had neutralized that of the other. Sometimes we had both been in one of the large closets together, I on a stepladder plowing through a pile of miscellany on the top shelf. "We don't want this any more," I would say, tossing something down on the floor. "Or this. Or this." And she, as these reminders of the past fell around her, would stoop and pick each one up, smooth it out, and place it lovingly among the things she wanted to keep.

"What in the world can you want with this?" I ask now, as I lean over and take out a little brown bottle that I remember throwing in the trash several days before. She takes it from me. "Why, hon, this medicine once saved your life. You fell down a long flight of stone steps when you were just three years old. That was when we were up in Chattanooga, and your daddy said that if it hadn't been for this medicine, you would've died."

"What is it?" I ask.

"I don't know. I think it's adrenaline."

"Well, it's no good now!"

"I know, but I think we ought to keep it."

"What for?"

"Well, it saved your life," she says, putting the bottle back in the suitcase. "We don't want to throw away any of our keepsakes."

She resumes her search, lifting sections of the contents of the suitcase here and there and peering in at the deeper layers. Presently she says something under her breath and begins untying the other old suitcase. It is filled with a similar assortment of souvenirs. She looks through it, without finding what she is looking for. Then she sits up straight. "Hon, where did we put that picture of your daddy?"

"Which one?" I ask.

"The big one in the oval gold frame. You know—the one on the wall over the piano."

"We left it there."

"*Left* it there?" she repeats incredulously.

"You can have the agent mail it to you if you want it," I say.

For a moment she sits quite still. Then a stubborn expression comes over her face, and hurriedly she ties up the two suitcases. When she has finished, she gets up and walks away. I call to her. She stops, comes back, and picks up one of her suitcases. I go to her and take her arm. "Mama, what's the matter?" I ask. "What are you doing?"

"Well, now, son, sit down and I'll tell you," she says. "I'll tell you what I've decided." She pats my hand as we sit down on the bench. "I've decided I won't go."

"You *can't* change your mind now!" I cry. "Everything's all set. We're about to get on the train."

"No, I've made up my mind," she says. "This is my home. All my things are here. I belong here."

"If *you* don't go, I can't go either," I say.

"Yes, you can, too. I wouldn't hold you back. It's right for you to go."

I look at the clock and swallow hard. "We've been through all this before," I say. "We've made the right decision. You've been very sick, and . . . "

"I know," she says, "and I'll never forget what you did for me. If you hadn't come home and looked after me, I'd not be living now. I'd . . . "

"That's not the point, Mama. Listen, please. Will you listen to what I say?"

"Yes, son."

"You're a lot better, but still not entirely well. You need a long rest. You know what the doctor told you. And I ought to go back to college."

"Yes, I know you should, hon."

"But the point is that you're not well enough to stay here alone."

"Why, yes, I am."

"There'd be no one to look after you if you got sick again. You wouldn't feed yourself properly."

"Yes, I will."

"You didn't the last time you were left alone."

"I've learned my lesson now."

"Mama, don't let's argue about it. It's all settled."

"But this is my home," she says. "What would I do in Marion? You mustn't worry about me, son. I've been looking after myself for a long time, and I certainly ought to know how by now."

"I'm not going to discuss it any more," I say irritably. "I'm sick of it. We've been round and round this for weeks. Every time I think it's settled, you change your mind. Then we go through the same old thing all over again. I'm through talking about it. If you won't go, then I have to stay and look after you—at least until I can find someone else to do it."

A man sits down across the way, stares at us, begins to read a paper. I scuff the sole of one shoe against the other.

"All right, son," she says finally. "I'll go."

For several moments we sit in silence. Then she says, more to herself than to me, "I think I saw the photograph album just now. Where was it?" Again she unties one of the old suitcases.

"You really must let me check them," I say to her.

She finds the photograph album and for a few minutes seems almost at peace as she turns its pages.

"Look, dear," she says, taking hold of my arm. "Do you know who that pretty little baby is?"

"No," I say, "but from the tone of your voice I gather it's me."

"Yes, it is," she says, and lapses into baby talk. "You were just the cutest, preciousest little baby there ever was. That's what you were!"

Gently disentangling myself from her grasp, I say, "You'd better let me close up this bag now." When I have retied the suitcase, I find her looking at a small, faded tintype. "Who's that?" I ask.

"Your daddy as a boy. See the date on it? It was taken in Monroe, in 1893."

She begins to cry. "How can I go?" she asks. "All my things are in my house. There's no other place to put them. Nobody else will ever take care of them—you know that. It'll never be the same after other people live there. They'll bang things up, be careless and destructful of the things we love!"

People are looking at her curiously. I am embarrassed.

"Don't feel so bad about it, Mama," I say in a low voice, putting my arm around her. "Of course there'll be some wear and tear, but you'll be getting rent. Maybe when you come back, you'll have enough money saved to fix the house up like you've been wanting. Anyway, we're not leaving anything that's valuable."

The words have little meaning for her, but she drinks in the kindness and seems comforted.

"I don't know what I'd do without you, dear," she says. "You're always so good to me."

"You'll be all right."

"I know I will," she says.

"Now, try to relax, Mama. It's almost train time. Don't look through the bags any more. Nothing has been lost."

"All right, dear." She folds her hands in her lap, as if making an effort to compose herself. Once, she leans forward to do something with one of the suitcases, but catches herself and sits up straight again. "You know, hon," she says presently, "we won't go on to Marion tonight. We're both tired. When we get to Shreveport, we'll go to a hotel and get a good night's sleep."

I feel a cold hand at my heart. "Mother! You know, don't you, that I'm not going with you?"

"Where are you going?" she asks.

"Mother! Pull yourself together, *please!* I'm going to Baton Rouge—to school. You know that."

"Oh, yes—yes."

I look away and take a deep breath, feel a mounting anxiety. I look at the clock. Another fifteen minutes. I have an intense longing to have it over.

She takes one of my hands in hers. "I wish you could go to Marion with me," she says. "After all, you need a vacation, too."

I extract my hand. "Are you sure you won't let me check two of your bags?" I ask. "It'd be a lot easier for you."

"You do whatever you think best, dear."

"I have to have your ticket," I say.

She gives it to me, and I pick up the two old bags. She holds my arm and looks at me as though she will not allow me out of sight. "I'll go with you," she says.

"No, Mother, please! You stay here with our other things. I'll be right back."

Reluctantly, she sits down. I feel her eyes following me as I cross the station. After checking the bags, I stand around the baggage room for a few minutes.

"You know," she says as soon as I return, "I've been thinking—and I've got an idea that seems very good to me."

"What is it?"

"Why don't I go to Baton Rouge with you? Instead of to Marion? We could rent an apartment with what we get from our house here. We'd be together and could look after each other. I could make a home for you. I'd like that."

"I don't think that's a good idea, Mother."

"Why not, hon?"

"Things are too uncertain. I don't want you to have to do housework and shopping and cooking. You need a long rest. There are a lot of reasons."

"We could make out all right if we were together," she says.

"No, I don't think it would be wise."

"Don't you want me with you?"

"Of course, Mother. I'm just telling you what I think best for both of us."

"I know you are," she says quickly.

"Come on, Mama," I say, unable to wait any longer. "I think I heard them announce your train. Anyway, we can get on now."

I pick up the three remaining bags, and we go down into the underpass and come up at Track Five, where her train is standing. The conductor, waiting beside the steps of the first coach, stands aside for us to board. She hesitates. I put my own suitcase on the platform and gently impel her forward, but she holds back.

"Go ahead, Mother."

She turns and catches the lapels of my coat, as though afraid of the train.

"Go ahead," I tell her. "I'll get on with you."

This magically overcomes her reluctance, and she climbs the steps. When we are seated on facing green plush seats, she leans forward with a worried expression, as if she can no longer put off telling me something of the greatest importance; yet she says nothing. Unable to avoid her eyes indefinitely, I force myself to look at her, and smile. She catches my hand in both of hers, presses it, caresses it, pleading mutely that I not go entirely away from her, that I save some part of my life and heart for her.

"Well," I say, "I guess it's about time for me to go."

She looks at me with eyes large and wet. "Be a good boy, son," she says. "I know you will. Get plenty of sleep, eat regular, wholesome meals . . . "

As she obviously has not finished, I wait, but she seems lost in thoughts of a different nature and does not continue.

The car is filling up. A woman with a baby sits down across the aisle from us. The baby is crying. A porter squeezes by our seats, carrying four handbags. A newsboy comes down the aisle hawking the *San Antonio Express*, and makes two sales.

"I really have to go now," I say. "This train is going to leave in a minute, and mine is, too. Well—good-bye, Mama."

I put my arms around her. Suddenly the thought of losing me seems to strike her with new force; she holds on to me and will not let go. I look down from my height on the white hair, and *I* feel agonizingly small. I loosen her arms gently and turn away. After a few steps down the aisle, I stop and call to her. "Have you got your ticket?"

She is looking at me and does not understand. "What? What's that?"

"Your ticket?" I say.

"My ticket?"

The expression of annoyance that sweeps over my face seems to make her comprehend.

"Oh," she says. "Oh, yes. You gave it back to me."

For a moment more, my glance meets hers. I try to smile affectionately; then I turn and quickly leave the car.

Passing her window on the outside, with my suitcase, I look up and see her eyes anxiously fixed on me through the glass. I smile, wave, and go on. After about twenty feet, I stop again, look back, and find that she has turned around in her seat, so as to follow me with her eyes until the last possible moment. I throw her a kiss. She returns the gesture with clumsy haste, dropping her purse as she does so.

I descend the steps to the underpass, come up again at

Track Six, and board the train that will take me to Houston, Lake Charles, and on to Baton Rouge. When I am seated, I glance out the window and, to my surprise, find that I can still see my mother. On adjacent tracks, the cars in which we sit are but a few feet apart. I see her clearly, and were it not for the layers of glass, could speak to her. She is still looking backward, in the direction in which I had gone. Her hands grip her purse tightly. She is wearing the old black dress that has been her Sunday best for so many years. When she turns and settles in her seat, I think surely she will see me. But almost immediately she looks back again, as if on the remote chance that I might reappear.

My train leaves first. As it begins slowly to move, it must have created for her the illusion that her train was moving—for she looks back more urgently, twisting her body, straining for one more glimpse of me. In this attitude of yearning, loss, and farewell, she disappears from my view.

IV

THE STRANGER

I HAVE COME to a strange land. I do not understand the language. The customs are peculiar.

At home I didn't have to think which path to take. One foot simply followed the other out into an average expectable environment to which I had a built-in adaptability. The unexpected could happen but remained the exception. Unthinking reactions had a natural fit with the way things were. In this land, fixed attributes of life have fallen loose and slanted. Familiar things are slightly twisted, have entered another dimension, and no spontaneous reaction of mine fits with anything. I must stay alert. I can never sleep. I have a terrible longing for home.

I AM POWERFULLY attracted by the girls of this strange land. I watch the dark, swinging curls as they bend over their work, the delicate features, the mysteriously swelling bosoms. Longing sinks into me like a knife, senses sicken, madness is not far away. Sometimes I think they are attracted to me, too, but in an easygoing, contented way, nothing like my panic craving.

Yet with all this watching, this jungle of fantasy, I don't really know what I want. To touch and to hold, to possess, to enter . . . but something more. The universe swings in the balance, and all hope of meaning, but whatever it is, I know I'm never to have it. My gaze locks on arched lips, on eyes in which for a breathtaking moment invitation flickers, on dark lashes that sweep down over glimpsed secrets. An abyss opens within me, sucks dry my throat. Heels click by on the pavement, skirt sways, brown eyes glance my way—suddenly she turns the corner and is gone, and I see, reflected in a store window, a face of hollow anguish.

A SUNDAY AFTERNOON long ago. I reach far back for this first glimpse of the forbidden. Jenny and I are playing in the living room while my mother, in the kitchen, visits with Jenny's mother.

My mother enters the room, smiles at Jenny, speaks to me. "We're going out for a while," she says, "won't be long. Your father is asleep. You must not leave the house. He might wake and need something, might call for me. If he does, tell him I'll be right back. I won't be long."

Jenny and I sit cross-legged on the floor. We are six years old, playing marbles for keeps. Light brown hair curtains her gray eyes and freckled face. She claims a marble not fairly won, I grab her hand, she stands up laughing, we struggle. The struggle becomes unbearably sweet. I cannot give it up. The plains of being are flooded with desire, everything is swept away, I utter in a voice suddenly hoarse the terrible word: "Let's fuck."

Childhood story

"All right," she says, and I am astonished at the ease and simplicity with which she immediately forgets the marble, lies down on the floor, pulls up her dress. I stand above her, look down on treasure suddenly mine, hesitate. An inward glance encounters an invincible prohibition that impales my conscience as heavy spear a leaping fawn. "No," I say, "let's don't."

"All right," she says. It's all the same to her, she's a summer day, carefree, wants to play. She stands. Curtains fall back in place over mysterious garden.

I COME FROM a line of tall and thin consumptives, and as a child seemed likely to continue the strain; you could count every rib. My grandmother encircled my skinny arm with worn fingers, regarded me sadly. "Son you must eat. You must put some flesh on those bones."

I heard a lot about this need for flesh on my bones. And a lot, also, about flesh in a different context. Throughout my childhood I sat on the rough benches of country churches in the South and stared up spellbound at a black storm of a preacher thundering about the sins of the flesh, the evil and the temptation of the flesh, the treacherous enticements of the flesh, which would sweep you away from God's grace into eternal hellfire. I believed but was mystified, and at home alone would flex my arm, observe the growing muscle, touch it, puzzled, unable to find in this flesh, which my grandmother said I should have more of, either dire evil or forbidden pleasure.

But some years later, as I lay abed of a spring night, the warm air drifting heavy with honeysuckle through the open window over my exposed body, my swollen member took on a life of its own, was taken over, rather, by a current of life that I thenceforth would bear forward as carrier rather than master, and in that current, as I at once realized, was both the delight and the evil of which I had been warned.

ONCE I WAS three weeks in a Boy Scout camp. In the woods by a river. About two hundred boys, twelve to fifteen, and a dozen counsellors, seventeen to twenty. We spent the days canoeing, rubbing sticks together, building fires, making arrowheads, earning merit badges. We had meals in the mess hall at long wooden tables. At one end of the hall was a raised platform where the Commandant and the senior counsellors ate. The Commandant was a tall man, stern and unsmiling, a retired army captain, walked about with a riding crop, always checking up on the counsellors, who were supposed to be always checking up on us. We slept four to a tent and there was to be no jerking off. The Commandant was determined to "stamp that out," gave talks on the dangers of "self-abuse." The camp was run along military lines, everything by bugle call. We got up to Reveille, went to bed to Taps. Most of us came from poor families. It cost ten dollars a week to be there, and a session was three weeks. Sunday was visiting day; families had the noon meal with us, spent the afternoon being shown around, left about five o'clock.

One Sunday evening we gathered for supper, seated ourselves at the long tables. The food was before us but we were not permitted to touch it until the Commandant said grace. He waited so long, glowering over our heads, we knew something was up. The counsellors shot warning glances at us. When the hall was completely still, the Commandant rose, but instead of pronouncing grace he began a little talk. It started off mildly enough, but from the beginning there was an ominous note.

"Last Sunday," he said, "I had the pleasure of meeting a lovely lady and her lovely daughter, the mother and sister of one of our Scouts. It was their first visit to our camp. I had the pleasure of having lunch with this lovely lady and her lovely daughter. We had a long, uplifting talk, and later I showed them about the camp. They met many of you and talked to you, were most interested in all the things we are doing here.

This lovely lady was particularly impressed by our goals and aspirations, by the high standards we seek to maintain, and by the ideal of honor which is the very heart of Scouting. I told her all these things with great pride, pride in this camp, and pride in all of you. . . .

"Now, I was very pleased, as you can imagine, to see this lovely lady again today. Also a little surprised, for she lives quite some distance and I had not expected her back so soon. She was alone this time, and one look at her told me this was no ordinary visit. In privacy and in great distress she told me what had happened. On Wednesday, the postman had delivered to her home a letter addressed to her lovely daughter. Fortunately, the daughter did not see it; the mother was able, by the grace of God, to intercept it."

He paused, scanned his audience with heavy portentousness. "She gave me the letter to read." Slowly he raised aloft the letter. "It was written by one of the Scouts in this camp." His face grew dark with passion, his voice throbbed. "It is the most odious letter I have ever read. It is a lascivious letter. It is a letter of vulgar language. It makes a vile proposal to that lovely girl. It is a disgrace to me personally and it is a disgrace to this camp." Slowly, he crumpled the pages in his fist. "Is Philip Orlikoff present?"

In the shocked silence that followed, the boy was gradually identified by the many who—curiosity, as at a hanging, gaining over horror—looked at him.

"Let him stand and come forward," the Commandant thundered.

The boy was at the back of the hall, near the door. He stood, hesitated, then uncertainly walked down the center aisle. With a gesture the Commandant directed him to mount the platform. They stood face to face. The boy could not bear the Commandant's gaze, his head fell. He was short and slight, his legs trembled. "Philip Orlikoff," the Commandant intoned, "you have brought disgrace upon this camp and upon all of your fellow Scouts. You have betrayed the solemn vows of Scouting. You have taken the Scout's honor and trampled it in mud and filth. You are a traitor. You are no longer a Scout." He snatched the emblematic blue kerchief from the boy's neck, ripped the merit badges from his shirt, threw them to the floor. "I am directing your local Scoutmaster, and also the national office, to strike your name from our rolls. I order you now to go directly to your tent, gather your belongings, and be gone from this camp within twenty minutes, never to return. You are dismissed."

The stricken boy descended the platform, came down the center aisle, his face white and taut. Everyone watched him, he looked at no one. The screen door closed behind him. He disappeared into the summer night. We never saw him again. The Commandant then raised both arms forward to shoulder level, closed his eyes. "Now may the grace of God be with us once again. Bless this food that now we take for the nourishment of our bodies. May we use our bodies only in pursuit of Thy purposes. Deliver us from temptations of the flesh. Amen."

You want a portrait of my superego? The Commandant is an exact copy. Vindictive, relentless. Implacable hatred of impulse. And would you want a snapshot of my id? It's that letter with its leering proposition, its dirty words, that letter in the Commandant's hand, like a mouse in the talons of a hawk. And my ego? You want that? Then you'll have the whole picture, what we psychoanalysts call the "tripartite psychic structure." My ego is Philip Orlikoff as he walks back down that aisle, bloodless, trembling, going out in disgrace into an endless night of alienation. So there I am, the whole of me, set forth in tableau, frozen in that mess hall drama of that long-gone summer evening. Scouting does in truth build character!

So, my dirty letters were never written, they remained but

fantasies. I was cowed by my own Commandant. I never propositioned anybody. Sex had to be redeemed by love, hallowed by marriage, before the Old Man would okay it. But now it seems that every time I passed up a sexual opportunity in the name of higher values, I was just cringing before the Commandant.

THE KNOWING MIND begins to know itself and to perceive, along with the freedom to do this or that, a horror about which it has no freedom at all. As soon as we become able, floating down the river of life, really to see the remarkable scenery and to enjoy the newly acquired freedom to move this way or that in the current, at just that moment we hear the roar of the cataract ahead. Amidst the luscious fruits, we see the coiled asp. We become, at one stroke, gods and food for worms.

A spring evening in a school auditorium during the rehearsal of a play. I am thirteen. I am weary of the farce, weary of the silliness of the cast, of our endless horseplay, mindlessness. A scene in which I have no part is being rehearsed; I stand in an open door at the rear of the dark and empty hall. A storm is underway. The door is on the lee of the building, and I step out under the overhang.

The rain swirls and beats. Lightning reveals a familiar scene in a ghostly light. I feel a sudden poignancy. Images strike my mind. The wind is the scream of a lost spirit, searching the earth and finding no good, recalling old bereavements, lashing the land with tears. And it was perhaps at just this moment I received my assignment, to search for meaning, an assignment variously perceived thereafter as sacred calling or as demons clawing at my back, anyway the task to which thenceforth the whole of my life would be dedicated—whether for better or for worse yet to be disclosed.

Consciousness leaves my body, moves out in time and space. I undergo an expanding awareness of self, of separateness, of time flowing through me, bearing me on, knowing I have a chance, the one chance all of us have, the chance of a life, knowing a time will come when nothing lies ahead and everything lies behind, and hoping I can then look back and feel it well spent. How, in the light of fixed stars, should one live?

I AM SEVENTEEN. The woman I love, ten years older, has told me never again to call her. I wander the streets of Baton Rouge. A drizzle of rain, the air motionless and chill. A day of vast silence, the drip of water, and, far in the distance, the disappearing sound of a car. Visions of violent acts, of tuberculosis, suicide notes.

I walk along a wall of gray brick topped in wisteria. Heavy purple blossoms hang beside my face. I stop before an iron gate, look into a garden of oleander, gardenias, roses. The heavy scents pour forth. Sinuous vertical bars rise above me to a filigree arch of vines, leaves, grapes. I grasp the bars, think: I will remember this moment. However long I live. Pain is branding it into my soul; the chill of wet iron, the flaking green paint, the whisper of rain, numb feet in wet shoes, the *drip, drip, drip*. My knuckles become white, my arms rigid. The pain swells, moves toward a more ample expression, perhaps a throwing back of my head and sobbing, perhaps a shaking of the gate till someone appears to love me, to drive me away, or to call the police.

Then there comes to me a thought, fully formed, coming not from the center of the pain but from a place slightly apart: *It is not necessary to suffer like this.* I stand still, startled, pursue the thought: I must be doing this to myself. The pain is given, but I am *choosing* to hallow it, to drive it toward some dark fruition, to walk for hours through a wet city, staring into forbidden gardens.

IN MY UNCLE'S house I felt inferior, the beneficiary of charity, tolerated rather than welcomed. I had not the money to ride the bus; I walked back and forth the three miles to the university. I was lonely. I knew no one and I was very shy. In classrooms and on the campus I saw many girls to whom I was attracted, but was too awkward and inhibited to approach or to speak. I was starving for recognition and acceptance, but held myself coldly aloof. I was intensely ambitious. I studied all the time, I made straight A's.

It's not quite true that I studied all the time, for during those years of loneliness and isolation I found solace in great novels: *Look Homeward Angel, The Magic Mountain, Anna Karenina.* I began to live more and more in the company of the people who inhabit these novels, I understood them, knew they would understand me. They came to seem more real than the people around me. I began to associate myself also with the authors of these wonderful books, to see myself in *their* company. A novel began to assemble itself in my mind. A novel about spiritual love and carnal love. About carnal love I knew nothing at all, but ignorance does not inhibit doctrine, and my novel, full of invidious comparison, was bent on establishing the supremacy of spiritual love. If true lovers would only love continently, their love would last forever. That my personal experience had been only with the spiritual kind did not, as I saw it, disqualify me for this task.

I decided to drop out of school and become a writer. But there were problems: I could not stay in my uncle's house if I were no longer in school, and I was unwilling to go back home. Real writers, I imagined, did not live at home with their mothers; they lived alone in great cities and had adventures.

My mother, in Marion, was very troubled. "Don't do it, son," she wrote to me. "Your education is the most important thing in your life. You must not interrupt it. Boys who drop out of college often never go back. Wait. This is premature. You're not ready to write a novel yet. You need more experience. It will be a better book if you write it later on."

Since my father's death it transpired that, in any conflict between my mother and me, I would always win, the only variable being how long it would take. In this instance, as always, I was patient, reasonable, and obdurate. She could not give me enough money, she wrote, for me to live independently. "Come back home," she urged, "come live with me in Marion." "I can live," I told her, "on whatever you can spare." She could perhaps manage forty dollars a month. "That will do," I said.

As a concession, I agreed to return to college after one year whether or not my novel were finished, confident that my writing career by that time would have accrued such promise that this commitment would not need to be honored.

So I traveled by bus from Baton Rouge to San Antonio and took a room at the YMCA, a room just large enough to contain a cot, a small table, and one straight chair. It cost five dollars a week, which left about the same amount for food. I found that I could get by on this and settled into a steady routine. I would get up early each morning, go down to the cafeteria for coffee and a roll, then back to my room to write until noon. After a similar break for lunch, I would write all afternoon. Having no money for pleasure or for vice, I worked also in the evenings. At ten or eleven, I would go to sleep. I held to this schedule every day, seven days a week. I knew no one, conversed with no one. I felt some pride in discovering that I could do this. The work went well, the story evolved smoothly, the pages of manuscript grew steadily thicker.

I was surrounded by many lonesome men, but made no friends. Occasionally I allowed myself a game of chess in the lobby, but for the most part was alone in my narrow room on the fourth floor, my life separate and untouched.

Throughout the fall and winter I worked steadily, ten to twelve hours a day. Page after page was covered with words, my two dozen pencils wore down to stubs, and the manuscript increased in bulk and weight. In the spring I became uncertain of its worth. I continued to work as before, but the inspiration was gone and the work was drudgery. I was caught in a morass of words. I wrote, rewrote, revised, and re-revised, but working over brought no improvement. I was struggling with something that would not stay put. A chapter which one week seemed good would, when read the next, seem worthless.

My mother's letters spoke more insistently of the necessity of my returning to college and of her inability to support me further in so uncertain a career as writing. Her brothers were scornful of my endeavor. "How is your son, the novelist?" Kleber asks her. "Is he sending you some of his royalties, or keeping it all for himself?" Often she asked when the novel would be finished, obviously looking forward to its completion, not as a significant accomplishment but as the end of a whim in which she had indulged me. There remained to be written only the two final chapters; unwilling to write them, however, while the value of those that preceded was in doubt, I had bogged down in the apparently endless task of revision. It was May and my time was running out.

One day I skipped lunch and used the fifteen cents meant for food to see a movie. *Anna Karenina*, with Greta Garbo, Fredric March, Basil Rathbone, Freddie Bartholomew. That was 1935; it all comes back: the sounds and smells of those days, the newspaper headlines, Mussolini, bombs falling on Ethiopia. I fell in love with Greta Garbo. Instantly, madly, deeply. I went to the theater every day, was swept away by that face. I began to feel that I must meet her, that we were meant for each other. Day by day it became more urgent that I find her, that something take place between us, that I make something known to her.

I wanted to rescue her. She was, I decided, of finer spiritual stuff than the world around her. As, of course, was I. Just as Vronsky, in the film, failed to appreciate her, so Hollywood, and America, were failing to appreciate her. But *I, I* understood her. And so could save her. Save her from that flaw in her nature that was leading her, repeatedly, to offer herself to unworthy men who would use and then reject her. With me it would be different. It was urgent that I reach her. She could not find me; I must find her.

So familiar

Longing swept away common sense. I scraped together enough money to buy a one-way ticket. The *Sunset Limited.* Two days and three nights. The flatlands of Texas and New Mexico, the deserts of Arizona, and then the sprawling vastness of Los Angeles, and a tiny room in a YMCA, and the grand project in my head.

It collapsed quickly. MGM would not give me her address or her phone number, but did tell me that she was in Europe and that no one knew when—or whether—she would ever return. Homesickness then and despair, and presently I'm back on the train, going back to Texas—three days without food, and plenty of time to reflect on my folly, on the dangerous gap between my visions and my abilities, staring out on the desert—empty pockets and empty stomach, and the shambles and all those now inglorious dreams.

BACK IN SAN Antonio, in the same room in the YMCA, I resumed work on my novel.

One night, having worked for thirteen hours, I went to bed at two in the morning. At five, attributing my insomnia to coffee, I got up and read. At eight, I went down to the cafeteria for breakfast. The morning passed quietly and profitlessly. Between ten-thirty and twelve I dozed in my chair. After lunch, having bolstered myself with more coffee, I bathed and prepared for work, but after a while gave it up.

With a sense of guilt I waited as the day passed, from my window watched the heat and glare of afternoon change to dusk and finally to cool darkness. At ten I went to bed, and at twelve was up again. While others slept, I went out in the city, drank coffee, and returned to my room. I forced myself to work, but for every sentence written, a half hour was spent dawdling. My mind would at one moment be empty, at the next full of irrelevant ideas. At five I surveyed my production and knew that the night, too, had been wasted.

The next morning was spent in one of the plush chairs in the lobby, dozing now and then. On arousing myself in the afternoon, I felt stuporous, my limbs stiff. After another futile attempt, I laid my writing aside, pondered the matter, decided that exercise might help, and set out immediately on a long walk. Reaching the suburbs, I spent an hour alternately running and walking, in order that the exercise would be sufficiently strenuous. Upon returning, I was thirsty and exhausted. After a hot shower I went to the cafeteria, but discovered I was not hungry. My only craving was for something cold. I could not recall ever having been so tired. Confident that I would sleep twelve hours, I went to bed early. Two hours later, I was still awake.

It occurred to me that I was trying too hard, that my fear of not sleeping was keeping me awake. I was afraid that I couldn't work if I didn't sleep, and I had to work. I tried to make my mind a blank. The void was quickly filled with sexual imagery. Presently, in disgust, I got up and began to read. With the subsidence of desire, weariness returned. At three, I went back to bed and counted sheep. At five, I slept, but woke in fright an hour later from a bad dream. I was relieved at having slept, and thought I would simply roll over and drop off again. But something prodded at me, unkindly, insistently. My novel . . . Could I ever straighten the thing out? Make it right? If I did not sleep, I would never be able to finish it. It occurred to me that the street light shining through the window might be keeping me awake. I lowered the blind and tied a handkerchief around my head. Again I was besieged with sexual imagery, and got up.

Perhaps it was overwork. I would take the remainder of that day for relaxation, would not think about writing. In the afternoon I played Ping-Pong and chess. At dinner I was vaguely disturbed by my inability to eat. In the evening I went to a movie alone. It didn't help, and another night passed sleepless. In the early morning I tried a method recommended by the room clerk, counting slowly, opening and closing my eyes with each count. "You'll never reach thirty," the clerk had guaranteed. At two hundred I could no longer move my eyelids, but could still count. A fit of coughing led me to wonder about tuberculosis.

I've got to sleep, I told myself. "You've *got* to sleep," I said, shifting to the third person, "if you don't sleep you can't write." I ordered myself to sleep, I *willed* sleep. I would sit at my table and try to write and find myself dozing, then an ice-cold shower and back to my room to try again. After a few minutes I would rest my chin in the palm of my left hand, elbow on the table, and would wake with a start just as my forehead was hitting the tabletop. I would then lie on my cot and instantly would be feverishly alert, agitated, tossing.

I lost weight, I looked bad, the woman in the cafeteria became worried about me. I was worried about myself. I needed help. I wanted to see a doctor, but was barred by my inability to pay. Then it occurred to me that Dr. Whittaker, who had attended my father in his final illness, who had treated also my mother, had never sent a bill and might see me also without charge.

After a long wait in his anteroom I was shown into his office. A tall man, elderly now, very thin, gray face, glinting glasses. He listened to my story, seemed puzzled, examined me, was still puzzled. "I don't find very much wrong," he said. I waited. He waited, uncertain. "But you *do* have infected tonsils."

"Could that be causing the insomnia?"

"I think it might. Do you have a sore throat?"

"No."

"Well, they *are* infected. It is a chronic, low-grade tonsilli-tis."

"What do you think I should do?"

"I think we'd better get those tonsils out."

Two days later, early morning at the hospital. A local anes-thetic which did not work. He injected me again . . . and again . . . and again . . . but still only a slight numbness. "Well, we just have to go ahead," he said.

I writhed and twisted in pain, and eventually he more or less scraped them out. He was called back to the hospital twice that day to cauterize my throat for bleeding. For a week I was groggy with pain and codeine, unable to eat except for ice cream.

But eventually even such a mauling heals, and after ten days my throat was functional again. I could at least swallow.

And the insomnia was unchanged.

In the lobby by a window, looking out on the street, I tried to think through my problem, to discover a cause. My eyes burned, my head ached, I was weak and tremulous. A girl walked by, a pretty girl, heels clicking on the sidewalk. As she passed from view at the end of the block, she reappeared immediately on the stage of my mind—without clothes. It occurred to me (a gift from my clever unconscious) that conti-nence might have produced an endocrine imbalance and that this, in turn, was causing insomnia. For some two hours I con-sidered sexual intercourse as a form of therapy, alternating between feverish excitement and abysmal guilt. Eventually I gave in to desire. My life was falling to pieces anyway, it would make no difference. At twelve noon, feeling myself a scoundrel, a sinner, and a fool, I left the Young Men's Christian Association for my first experience of what, in my novel, I called "carnal love." The prostitute was a silent, dull-witted Mexican girl, the heat was stifling, the circumstances were sordid, the price was cheap.

An hour later, back in the YMCA lobby, I sat down to analyze the experience, but found that there was little to think about, nothing to conclude. After a while I went upstairs to my room and lay on my bed. Too nervous to lie still, I returned to the lobby and spent the afternoon playing chess.

My exhaustion was now extreme. Lying down, I would toss and tumble. Standing, I would be dizzy. I would go out to walk, hoping to replace sick exhaustion with normal fatigue, but after a few brisk steps I would slow down, falter, would lean against a building to rest, would then recover consciousness to find myself, legs buckling, slumping toward the pavement.

I was getting sick, didn't know what to do, would have to go back to see Dr. Whittaker. But just then I was overtaken by a wave of common sense. Don't be a fool, I said to myself. Don't be a fool *again*. You *knew* that tonsillitis was not causing this trouble. Why did you let him butcher you?

That night I stood for a long time in a hot shower while through my mind there ran a refrain: "I've got to sleep. I've got to sleep. If I can't sleep I can't work. I've got to sleep." At midnight I got up and tried to read, but drifted off into daydreams. At two o'clock I lay down again, telling myself that I did not care whether I slept or not. Images of violence came to mind: I saw myself striking, slashing, piercing—machine-gunning a multitude in a narrow street. Four o'clock found me still awake. Too much on edge to stay in bed, I dressed and went out. With only slight exertion my heart beat painfully, giving me a sense of threatened suffocation.

Never had the city seemed so deserted or lonely as it did now in the gray light. For blocks no person could be seen. The only vehicles were an occasional cab or milk wagon. A surprising number of cats loitered aloofly in the closed entrances

of shops, arching their backs against unfriendly doors, mew-
ing as I passed, waiting unhappily for shopkeepers to open
their stores. There was a faint, cool mist in the air, which soft-
ened the outlines of buildings and obscured some of the dirt
and stains of the city. After a while I stopped on a corner to
watch the sunrise. Across the street was a hospital, from one
of the windows of which a nurse looked out at me for a
moment, then disappeared. I could hear the sounds of breakfast being prepared, drifted off into a fantasy of being a doctor,
bending over a hospital bed, listening to the heart of a critical-
ly ill child.

Back in the YMCA, the smell of doughnuts and eggs
repelled me. I ordered only coffee, and on lifting the cup, was
surprised at the tremor of my hand. Drinking in sips, I sat
there in a daze. The taste of sugar and cream nauseated me.
On reaching the toilet, I vomited. Feeling weak and sick, I
slowly mounted the four flights of steps to my room. My eyes
stung. Looking in the mirror, I saw that they were bloodshot
and sunken. My face was haggard. My trousers hung loosely
about my hips.

Sitting on the edge of the bed, I wondered how long this
had been going on. Twenty-six days, I discovered on counting
back. The information lay inertly in my mind. I felt capable of
neither reason nor feeling. The refrain, "I've got to sleep. If I
can't sleep I can't work," ran round my mind. Too tired to
undress, I lay down fully clothed, but could not lie still. It was
as though something were forcing me to twist and turn and
roll, making of the attempt to sleep an agony of restlessness.
After a few minutes, unable to endure it any longer, I got up
and sat at my desk.

It was eight o'clock. Another day was beginning. A day like
the last. A day of nausea, nervousness, and paralyzing fatigue,
of chess and movies and cheap magazines, a day which would
end at last in a night like the one just finished.

I bit my lip and struck the table with my fist. Repeatedly, slowly, I pounded the table in rhythmic fury. The muscles of my back contracted. My head was drawn back, my feet pressed hard against the wall, my chest constricted. It occurred to me that I was going to have a convulsion. Obscurely I felt that I was acting, and that I could stop it, but was not sure I wanted to. One of the blows missed the tabletop, my knuckles grazing the edge. With the pain I regained control of myself, and after a moment was able to relax.

I extended my fingers, watched drops of blood stand out, realized that I had reached an extremity of trouble. As the problem had become more serious, my ability to deal with it had diminished. Now the need was urgent. Not much time left. I wondered if there were something wrong with my mind.

In the public library I looked in the card catalogue under "Insomnia." Nothing. Under "Sleep." *The Sleeping Beauty.* Under "Psychology." There I found many books. I browsed through them all day, found nothing relevant, and the second day found nothing. But on the third day I came upon an idea that felt like a psychological tool. I was reading a case history. A young man with a paralyzed right arm went from doctor to doctor. Nothing wrong could be found. There was no explanation for the paralysis. Finally he came into the hands of someone who inquired, not just into his symptom, but into his life. He was a student of theology, deeply religious, and had for some months been in extreme conflict about masturbation.

Here was a stunning idea: Something from which one suffers, for which one seeks relief, something which appears as an affliction, alien to any need or intent, perhaps even life-threatening, may nevertheless be created unconsciously as a solution to a psychological problem. Created and maintained by the one who suffers from it.

Could I be doing that? Could I be creating this insomnia for an ulterior purpose to which I was choosing to be blind? It seemed unlikely. If I can't sleep I can't write. If I can't write I can't finish my novel. But finishing the novel is what I most urgently want to do. It didn't seem to fit. I dropped the tool, left the library, and started back to the YMCA, defeated, baffled.

But continued to think about that young man, that theology student with a paralyzed arm. I felt some kinship with him. The refrain circled in my mind: If I can't sleep I can't . . . finish my novel.

Could it be that I *believe* I want to finish it, but that something in me of which I am not aware wants just the opposite? Why? What could possibly be the intent?

So I will never have to recognize that it is a failure.

Then an explosion of insight. Six weeks ago, when I read through my manuscript, I had recognized it to be worthless, but had suppressed that recognition because it would have demanded a painful revision of self-image. I would have had to see myself as immature and grandiose. To avoid that revision, I was willing to make myself sick.

Suddenly I saw the complete scenario: If I can't sleep I can't write, I will become exhausted, no cause will be found, I will lose weight, become weak, tuberculosis will be suspected, I will be sent like Hans Castorp to a sanitarium, recovery will be slow, and in the midst of all this trouble my unfinished novel will be forgotten, and I will never have to acknowledge that it was no more than a sentimental and self-indulgent account of a hypersensitive boy written by an immature author.

Back in my room I sat down to my table, this time to undertake a different kind of writing.

Dear Mama,

You were right, I was wrong: I'm not ready to write the novel I had in mind. It is almost finished, but I am not going to finish it because I know now that it is a failure. I'm going back to college. . . .

That night I slept soundly. I never saw Dr. Whittaker again.

Recognized failure & it relaxed him

V

PSYCHOANALYSIS

I AM NINE years old and am bullied by the other boys. As we stream out of school, they tug at my clothes, trip me; one confronts me in unexpected friendliness as another kneels unnoticed behind me. A bad time. Always toppled backwards.

One day I encounter Roy, my archtormentor, on a deserted road. He drops a loop of rope over my head. "Nice tie," he says, takes the short end, and yanks as, with his other hand, he forces the knot into my throat. We scuffle. He slaps me. I push, he falls. When he gets up, he has become serious: I have been aggressive, that's what he wanted; I have given him license; now he need not hold back. I see in his face a surging zeal. I flail and retreat; he moves in. Unexpectedly, I land a blow that interferes with his breathing, and immediately press my advantage, hit him in the face. He throws up his left arm, I hit him in the ear.

I am moving forward. Now *I* feel the fierce joy. What my father has done to me, I can do to another. I land my fist in his midriff; he reels back. A different expression comes to his eyes. Fear, that despicable thing, that cravenness uniquely my own—it has leapt from me to him. There it is, *mine*, in his eyes. And with that leap we are transformed: I now am the brave one, he the coward. I push him back. He twists away, I deliver a rain of blows.

And now I encounter in myself something new, something other than bravery: I have *become* my father, I am going to crush him. I feel deep joy. I grab him by the shirt, jerk him toward me; he sees my fist coming at his eye; his face crumples. I hesitate. Predator with partially mangled prey, what shall I do? He has been tormenting me, why not take revenge? Delight in it? He begins to cry.

The paths diverge. I look both ways. I see myself more truly in Roy's fear than in my father's fury. I let him go.

I did not fight again. Often with longing and with loss I remembered the fierce delight, the exultant moving in for the kill. I went the other way, found my place and my work among those who are afraid. I understand them better. I help them be less afraid. I cannot help myself.

IN AUSTIN, TEXAS, in the thirties, I could hear from Europe the premonitory rattle of war, could anticipate its spread across the Atlantic. Able-bodied, without children, a failing artist, nothing to excuse me from the coming draft, I would be a front-liner. I could already feel the bayoneted rifle in my hands, my revulsion at using it, my fear of having it used against me.

I discovered in myself an interest in medicine. As Hitler moved into Poland, I moved into the College of Physicians and Surgeons of Columbia University. Cowards often manage to appear brave: On Saipan and Okinawa I was a battalion surgeon with the Marines, it seeming but by mere chance I had nothing directly to do with rifles and bayonets.

SEVERAL PEOPLE LOVE me. Many think highly of me. Were you to ask, they would tell you of my kindness, intelligence, generosity, empathy. And offer little by way of qualification—other than that I am difficult to know.

Viewing myself, I see a different person, find no ground for love. Anxious, self-centered, tormented, weak. Too bad. I would have it otherwise, would wish for the noble features others ascribe to me. But I know myself better than they, make reference to a range of thought and feeling, of motivation and behavior, unavailable to them. Even those closest to me can know but a fraction of what I know. I've really got the dirt on me.

Since I intend in this work the utmost honesty, the reader, if I am successful, cannot in the end think well of me. If he or she does, I will have failed.

Is this credible? Is not every book written in the hope of love? Could any writer knowingly undertake such candor as would call for rejection?

Well . . . stranger things have happened. And anyway, there's no end to my deviousness. Perhaps I'm angling for some kind of meta-acceptance; perhaps I hope the style with which . . . Enough!

ONE MUST BEND the world to fit one's needs or bend one's needs to fit the world. If one cannot, by force or daring or skill, get what one wants, one must turn upon oneself and change what one wants.

The bending of self is renunciation. But needs die hard. We can renounce the having, but not the desiring. The hungry nose against the glass of the patisserie; the young man alone, alone, on the windy street, seeing, as the Mercedes takes the corner, the pretty girl fling herself across the driver and kiss him on the mouth. What can one do with that? It won't go away. One is stuck with it, bitten by it, one turns it over and over, endlessly, the worm of envy burrows deeper, and it comes presently to seem that this agony of heart is unique, that it has never happened this way before, that it should be rendered in words.

And then—who knows?—the novel about to be begun may prove a masterpiece. In fantasy one is planning to change the world: one will be acclaimed, honored, sought after by beautiful women; and there, at that imagined future moment, flowers the love that in the present one has not the nerve to seek. In the present it is hidden, out there somewhere perhaps, but withheld; one would have to go knocking on doors; but in that illusory future it will be lavished. One will have changed the world one lives in by literary accomplishment.

My own next effort at a novel was titled *Come Away*—from Yeats.

> Come away, O human child!
> To the waters and the wild
> With a faery, hand in hand,
> For the world's more full of weeping than you can understand.

Too full, anyway, to notice me; my gift is declined. I keep trying. Ten years later I am still at it. This time it is called *The Elusive Anguish*; but the longed-for fame proves more elusive than the anguish. Everything fails. I am in a cage with invisible bars. I keep trying but see no new way of trying, and so lose hope.

Failure twists the head around, forces the gaze inward, moves toward inquiry, insight. It moves me toward psychoanalysis.

THE NOON LECTURE. It is 1946, Topeka, Kansas, the Winter Veterans Administration Hospital. We wait, one hundred psychiatric residents, all young doctors just home from the war. Disillusioned with politics, with medicine, we want to live in the realm of psychodynamics.

Dr. Knight is three minutes late. The room falls silent as he enters. He is our most admired teacher; we accord him a hushed respect and attention.

He proceeds to the front of the room, takes papers from his briefcase and places them on the table, faces the class. A large man, powerful shoulders, gray hair, ruddy complexion, pale blue eyes. He starts to speak, pauses, straightens his tie, tightens the knot, adjusts the handkerchief in his coat pocket, straightens his notes on the table, starts to speak, pauses. Again he straightens his notes, this time seeming intent on having them exactly in the center, each side of the notepaper parallel with the corresponding side of the table. The class watches with curiosity, then astonishment. At the first tittering, he cuts the scene, sits behind the table. "Tell me what you have observed and what you can infer from it."

Since the announced topic of his lecture is obsessive-compulsive mechanisms, this is easy; two or three hands go up immediately. The first speaker gives a description of the behavior in terms of measuring, balancing, making symmetrical. He is stuck at the surface, will never be an analyst. The next speaks of the ambivalence of obsessional states, unconscious hostility being opposed and balanced by a precisely equal counterforce. Another identifies the motivating impulse as anal, and says that this origin, at the source of all dirtiness, explains why the defense takes the form of excessive neatness. Dr. Knight listens without reaction, calls impassively on one person after another. Presently my friend Jeff Monroe begins to rock slightly in his chair, coughs, clears his throat, grins, shoots up his arm.

"The Menninger Clinic keeps you very busy," he says. "You've probably seen four patients this morning, had a couple of hallway conferences, a dozen phone calls, and no time to think about this lecture or even to open your mail. You finish with your last patient at eleven-fifty and have just ten minutes to get across town. You drive fast, feel tense, resentful. Walking down the hall, you look at your watch, know you are late—so there's no time now even to stop and pee . . . and we must seem to you like a nest of hungry birds, mouths gaping, waiting to be fed. And just then the obsessional routine occurs to you. 'Let *them* do some of the work for a change.' And we have. We've given a quarter of your lecture. You seem now to have caught your breath, to be rested, and perhaps ready to take over the rest."

There is general laughter. I scribble a note and pass it to Jeff: "Now he won't say anything!"

"Are there other comments?" Dr. Knight asks. When there is no response, he stands, moves to the lectern. "I had meant to say something about my behavior," he says, "but I guess it has been pretty well covered. So, let's proceed—"

"Please excuse this interruption," I say, without asking permission. Dr. Knight looks up disapprovingly. "My interpretation of your foreplay to this lecture had to wait until you began talking . . . because it included the prediction that you would not say anything about it."

There is a moment of apprehensive silence. The pale blue eyes settle intently on me; he is trying to remember my name.

"You meant for your obsessional routine to be discussed at the level of the lecture you are about to give—a model of the sort of thing you're going to talk about. And that's where most of the comments have been pitched. Jeff's remarks went below that level, took you by surprise. You were amused— impressed, too, for they were accurate—but also uncomfortable, and hence annoyed. He was undressing you in public. So why did you not put him down? Because . . . the heart of analysis is to look elsewhere—to be presented with experience which the patient means to be understood at one level, but to see the significant motivation to lie at quite another level, in an area the patient does not want you to notice. And that's exactly what Jeff did with you. And for a student to do that to a professor is impertinent; but since you had presented us with a bit of clinical behavior and asked for an interpretation, you inadvertently gave him license to do just that, and so could not pull rank and put him in his place. But still it irks you; it was an invasion—particularly that part about no time to pee. So, how can you punish him? Why, by not replying. By denying him the satisfaction of your admission that he was right. That is to say, *by behaving exactly like a resistant patient* who reacts to a correct but discomfiting interpretation with a brief silence, then changes the subject.

"All this, of course, raises the question of how you will react now to these comments of mine—and I have some ideas about that, too, but won't tell you because the telling would enable you to react otherwise . . . to punish *me!*"

For a few moments there is a dreadful silence. Then Dr. Knight smiles slightly, and a ripple of nervous laughter flutters across the room.

"With your permission and indulgence, Dr. Monroe, and yours, Dr. Wheelis—and if the punishment does not seem too harsh—I would like to get on with my lecture. For whatever you may think to the contrary and however rushed I may have been, I do have something to say, even some notes."

WE WERE SHOWING off, leaping through the reductive hoops of the new analytic game. We wanted to get into the Institute. All of us in this room were going to be psychiatrists, but few would become analysts. We wanted to be noticed.

And I *was* noticed. Afterward, in the hallway, another resident said to me, "Boy, are you in trouble! Might as well pack your bags." But that was envy. Everyone knew that I was in.

The age of psychology was beginning, and I had just stepped on the bandwagon.

And so was able, presently, to ask Dr. Knight to read my novel, that cross on which I had been hanging for years. After a few weeks, he called me to his office. "I don't think you can correct what's wrong with this book," he said, "until you are analyzed." Whatever else he said is forgotten, but there it was, in that one sentence, the mysterious glittering promise: Effort is unavailing; the underlying psychic mechanism must be explored. Then, *then!*, all will be possible.

A LARGE ROOM. The spines of books splash across the walls a riot of color, a profligate diversity of worlds. Unwavering white light, a north wall of glass. The windows are closed, the lace curtains hang still. A room of immense quiet, of inquiry. Inquiry beneath the available answers.

The room is soundproof. The doors are doubled. The world cannot hear what is said here nor see what is done here, though, in fact, nothing is done in this room. Action is not permitted.

Along one wall a low couch. Behind the couch a massive black leather analytic chair. Between the two a teak cabinet— perhaps a barrier.

Pictures by Edvard Munch, the sad unbridgeable distances between men and women.

VI

GIRLS

I FEEL THE ache of love, the unquenchable burning. It seeks union, will be satisfied by nothing less than everything. Nothing can put out this fire, it will burn on and on within me until I am left in ashes. The only cure is the waning of love that follows upon the fusion that love so insistently demands.

WHENEVER WE BURN with that hard, gemlike flame, we have illusorily found our heart's desire in the beloved. In the rain of conflicts to come our papier-mâché angel will turn into a witch or a drab. Yet this passion for a falsified other may be the only thing in life really worth while. Without it, one lives in a world of dailiness. The love possible in that world is hearth love, the ordinary love of husband and wife, of parent and child, of friends. This love may be constant, caring, loyal, may protect against anxiety, may provide the only security possible in a world of hazard, all these good things, and it may be, if we were wise, we would settle for it, renouncing that fever in the blood; but it does not transcend, does not lift us up and out, does not take us to the other side.

THE LAUGHING GIRL in the bikini under the red and blue umbrella, the willowy girl with the doe eyes and generous mouth at the cocktail party—crystallization points of a passionate preoccupation. Of what nature? Not a vision of giving, of coming to know the needs of such a girl and of meeting those needs. That's what love is, but is no part of this wild yearning. I'm concerned with getting. What do I want?

Whatever it is, I must give up hope, must try rather to want to give. But I wish I knew what it is I want, so deeply, so vainly, before I give up wanting it.

LONG LINE AT the bank. Four tellers. This will take about ten minutes, I estimate. Take my place at the end of the line, begin reading my newspaper. I move forward, one or two steps at a time, newcomers fall into place behind me. One of the tellers, I observe, is a trainee; an experienced teller sits beside her, supervising. Avoid her, I tell myself, she will take forever. I look at my watch, am nearing the head of the line, will pass up my turn if it is she who becomes available to me. Yet my gaze is locked on her.

She wears a sleeveless sweater of muted colors over a white blouse; dusky skin; holds herself quite erect, an air of dignity. A supple neck, like the curving stem of a tulip, extends upward from the white collar, blossoms into . . . no, not blossoms, not yet, she's too young. Buds, rather, a dark tulip bud. Full lips, slender nose, large eyes.

I am at the head of the line now, the supervisor points out something to her, she smiles, is grateful for instruction. Her manner is both warm and shy. Her customer nods and leaves. She looks up at me. And at the same moment the teller beyond her is also free, calls out, "Next!" I walk forward quickly, can now pass her by without implication of rejection, yet am stopped abruptly, as by a brick wall, impulse subverting intention. I stand before her, breathing fast.

"How is it going for you?" I ask, sliding forward some checks to be deposited. Large eyes set widely apart, a rather dark blue. Long, curving eyelashes. Reserve, restraint, great dignity. A waif, but like the daughter of a king. Her hair is dark, falls below her shoulders. "Oh, *very* well," she says, grateful for my goodwill with its promise of patience with her inexperience. Correct pronunciation but definite accent. The three words hang in the air like musical notes, quiver, dazzle me. She begins checking over the deposit slip. "Is this your first day?" "Oh no," she says, "I'm starting my second week." Again that musical reverberation. Her words touch me like fingers, light, cool, caressing. Exotic accent. My mouth is dry. "Are you Scandinavian?" "No—" she hesitates, a slight faltering. "Persian."

Persian? Ah, Iranian. An exile from home, an enemy here. Persian is a plea, means, "Do not condemn me. It is not I who held your hostages." Poor kid. Probably has no money; the blouse is inexpensive, the sweater handknit. The supervisor is pointing out something to her. She listens seriously, conscientiously, wants to learn, feels lucky to have found this job. Suddenly I am ashamed of the large sum I am depositing. She probably has nothing. Slender waist, wears dark pants. She is giving me a receipt. "Thank you," she says. My business with her is over. I can find no reason to stay. "I hope it goes well for you here," I say. "Oh, thank you." She blushes.

I walk away, out of the building, sit in my car, staring, do not turn on the ignition, have forgotten my rush, where I was going, the pressure of time. A pain spreads out in me as if I would die. I try to argue it away, bring back her face. Fragile, vulnerable, poised. Beautiful, to be sure, but why am I so affected? What about her breasts? Did I notice? Can't remember. Probably small. Something slim and boyish about her. And so young. Iranian is a bad word; of course she's Persian. Something terribly decent in the way she said it, with but the slightest hesitation; wants to disclaim connection with the Khomeini tyranny, yet not deny her origin.

I move my head from side to side in a torment of longing. Try to shake it away. Why such desperation? She is indeed beautiful, but some beautiful faces leave me unmoved. Is it that pliant vulnerability, that hint of receptivity, that she might yield to my intention, be shaped by my will, a Galatea waiting in marble for my chisel? My urgent, throbbing chisel! Words! Words! That exotic face, that slim form, have entered my heart, set me afire. I start the car, roar away as if to have done with her, to leave her behind. To no avail. She has knifed into my heart. She goes with me.

WHAT CAUSES THE world to have meaning? And what causes that meaning to drain away? What leads us to be attached to the world, and what causes those attachments to falter? Like the water table beneath a flourishing land, sex nourishes the life above it. From it derive not only fields of wheat, tall trees, green meadows, but also the play of children, the sound of ax and saw. When it drains away, the life above it dries up, withers, is gone with the wind.

IN THE BOOKSTORE the paperback fiction is arranged alphabetically by author. After Sherwood Anderson comes Anonymous, that great master of erotica. *The Boudoir, A Man with a Maid, My Secret Life.* (Jane Austen, on the other side, shrinks back, offended.) All of the great works of literature are arrayed here before me, from Agee to Zola, all available for uplift of soul, but I stand rooted before that hypnotic master Anonymous. I take a volume from the shelf. It's not difficult to find a detailed, explicit passage. I read to the end, two or three pages at most, return the book to the shelf, take out another. I handle the books with care, intent not to soil a cover or crease a page; for I will not buy, would not own such a book, take it home, no more than a heroin addict, trying to stop, would have a supply of drug in the house. I am yielding to a vice, but only for a moment, will not surrender to it. To possess such a book, read it leisurely, start to finish, leave it on my night table, shelve it in my bookcase—that fullness of violation is beyond me. Mine is a hit-and-run encounter, I read quickly, one or two passages, hold the book apprehensively, guiltily, know myself to be in bad faith; for I am not really above this stuff as I would like to think, nor am I an honest customer. I am a pretender, am making an unauthorized loan—I am a thief of lust!—therefore feel barely tolerated here, increasingly sensitive to the comings and goings of clerks, suspect that each one as he passes identifies the passage being read. I shrink back against the shelves, try not to block the passageway. My mouth becomes dry. I have reached my limit. I replace the book, move on. To diffuse the specificity of my interest I pause in brief dissimulation before Moravia and Updike, then leave the store.

I turn west up Clement Street into the wind. There is a metallic taste in my mouth, a weak and empty feeling in my stomach. This isn't it. I feel soiled and corrupt, am further away from it now than before. Life is a treasure hunt, I have to play, there isn't anything else, but I am being given mischievous clues: "Find a pearl in the outhouse."

AT MY DENTIST'S office, a woman in the waiting room. Had been brushing her hair, stopped as the door opened. She now replaces brush and mirror in her handbag, opens a magazine.

She is sitting by a table lamp, her hair luminous in the glow. I sit in a corner, unobtrusively, to observe her. She is very beautiful. I begin to feel the familiar pain. And she is young enough, I think mournfully, to be my daughter. No, the other way round: I am old enough to be her father; for I would not want her any less young. Slender and—I take the measure of her long legs—tall. The legs are stockinged and crossed, high heels. Silk dress, mauve. Why so dressed up? Maybe a first visit. Her hair is dark, silky, a disarray of planned abandon. Her face is not happy, not serene, but has a noble perfection of line, a natural reserve and dignity—and a latent turbulence, something somber, brooding, passionate.

She feels me looking at her, glances up with a frown. I am in a storm of exaltation and despair. Here I am again, I think wildly, at the same old place: the gates of heaven, without key or password, without entry, without innocence. What do I want with her? Inwardly I plead: Don't go away! . . . But in a minute the door will open and *I* will go away. What is she doing here at *my* hour? Have I made a mistake? No, she. Or maybe she is Dr. Orrick's daughter, here to see him for a minute during the break. No, no, not his daughter. Too dressed up, too much on edge, too much like me. She's a patient. Oh God, I don't want her to go. What can I say?

"Excuse me, are you here to see Dr. Orrick?"

She looks up reluctantly—slight offense at the intrusion. "No."

Didn't get very far with that. What else can I say? What do I *want* with her? What, if I had her, would I do with her? My heart, with each caged and desperate beat, flutters out a wordless code of misery.

"Was afraid I'd made . . . a mistake," I say lamely. She does not look up. I'll give up my time, I think. I'll sit here and watch her. I won't leave her. From Dr. Orrick's office comes the sound of voices, footsteps. The young woman closes her mag-

azine, now eagerly, perhaps anxiously, expectant. The time is
at hand.

Nothing happens. The silence grows heavier. I cannot recall
my devouring gaze. It makes her nervous. I feel a vast and desolate hunger, want to know her in most intimate detail, all that
has happened to her, her entire life. Why is she here? What
does she suffer? Does she have a toothache? I visualize the
tooth, her tongue touching it gingerly. Then *my* tongue enters
the dark red cavern, caresses the tooth. Is she alone? Whom
has she loved, why has it not worked out? If it had been me, it
would have worked out. I would never have left her. What does
she fear? What does she desire?

The door opens. A man appears. Bushy hair. Pinstripe suit,
navy blue. The young woman is on her feet, smiling, locks
arms with him. They leave together.

SEX IS OUR tie to the world, the source of meaning. It drives
us out of ourselves into engagement with the world. Because
it is the nature of this drive to endow another—an *other*—with
importance. And since this important other, becoming ever
more enticing, spellbinding, this eventually supremely valuable other, lives and moves out there in the world, among the
people and patterns and practices of the world, and because it
is there she must be sought if ever she is to be found, the world
itself, its forms and patterns and practices, has value and we
attend to it.

PREOCCUPIED WITH ANNETTE. Lovely Annette. Yet do not
know her, have seen her but once, at the tennis courts, have
spoken to her only a few words, would not recognize her on
the street. Nevertheless, nevertheless . . . my desires clamor
hungrily after her cloudy image like hounds after a fox.

What I pursue, endlessly, is not *out there* in *her*—in any
her—but in me. It is a vision of love of which I comprise one

half and seek forever the other half. What I project onto her is a longing reciprocal to my own. It is my own longing experienced as coming back toward me. What I desire so desperately, I already have. It is in me, my very own. Only aimed in the wrong direction, an arrow flying outward from my heart toward some other, while I yearn that it come flying from some other back to me. Where is that lover who will send her arrow into my heart—that I may die of love?

What started this was my phone call last night, a brief exchange to arrange a tennis game. Her "Hello" was neutral; I identify myself. "Oh yes!" She laughs, slight embarrassment; the timbre of voice, the quality of laugh, is warm with that kind of recognition that indicates she has been thinking of me. That's enough. Just that. I am instantly persuaded that a gleaming arrow such as the one I hold so restlessly, so ready and so eager to aim, is forming itself in her and aiming at my heart.

This is not love. Love is the caring that two people manage to negotiate between their yearnings to be one and the conflicts that would drive them apart. What I feel is pure yearning. There is no *other* out there. My Annette is a phantom. The real Annette is unknown to me, and when she comes to be known will disappoint me.

THE AGITATION OF this yearning will drive me to madness. How much can one endure? I am a magnet in a world of wood, of ivory, of diamonds, cardboard, and snow. But no metal! No metal! Will I never feel that rushing together? that flying into one another's arms, that binding together, that blinding fusion, wholeness?

 DESIRE INCREASES WITH despair: measure the one, you measure also the other. Hunger for women grows as the capacity to satisfy it diminishes.

Isaac Bashevis Singer: " . . . hell is made up of yearnings. The wicked don't roast on beds of nails, they sit on comfortable chairs and are tortured with yearnings."

ANNA, MY FIRST real love. We were nineteen. We sat on the ground and leaned against a tree, shoulders touching, fingers intertwining. Children waded in the brook, laughed, mothers called. We took off our shoes, tunneled our toes under matted needles. The red sun on the horizon palisaded the grove of pines with golden pales. We looked in each other's eyes, talked about ourselves, understood many things. The afternoon was ending, people were leaving. Darkness came. No sounds now but the locusts and the brook, no light but the fireflies—bright periods on the dark page before us. We lay on the ground, and when we talked we whispered. She did not push back my hands, seemed to feel that what I felt was good.

It was late when we came from the park. The houses were dark. From far away came the sound of a speeding car, a whining menace spreading in the still night. Coming from darkness, we blinked in the glare of a street light. Thousands of locusts in a teeming halo swarmed about the light, flew against it, fell to the still-warm sidewalk.

Through a long hot summer we went often to the park. In August, her manner changed, her face darkened. I had forebodings, dreams of losing her. She laughed at my gloom, but with a hollow note. Her parents took her away for a vacation. I walked the streets waiting, counted hours, checked off days. When she returned, her eyes were swollen; she would not look at me. When finally she told me, I was relieved, had feared something worse. I wanted to marry her but she would not. We found the name of a doctor in another city, invented a story for her parents, went by train.

The waiting room was dirty. A sign on the desk informed us we should ring the bell and wait. We sat on an old sofa, which responded with a cloud of dust and the twang of a broken spring. There was but one window, morning sunlight falling on a begrimed pane. The door opened and a Mexican girl came out, glanced at us furtively. Presently the doctor appeared, a heavy man in a surgical gown. With a gesture he invited us in, explained the procedure. "I've found it best," he said, "to collect my fee in advance." I gave him the money, which he tucked away under his gown. With sudden helplessness I watched him take her into an inner room. When she came out, she walked very slowly. At the hotel we tried to look grown-up, registered under false names, felt like thieves.

She slept for a while, restlessly, talking in her sleep, awoke feeling better. The day passed with a terrible slowness. Nothing happened. She telephoned her parents, invented a reason for getting back late. I called the doctor, who protested but agreed finally to see her. He did not carry a bag and there was nothing physicianly in his manner. "Spread your legs," he said, pulling on one rubber glove. He lifted her skirt and examined her brusquely, as she stood there by the door. She gasped and clutched the wall. "It'll come," he said. "Just give it time."

But we had no time. And no money. Our alibis were used up and we had to go back. Somehow I got her aboard the train and into a lower berth. She kept smiling and saying she was all right, squeezing my hands very hard. The Pullman was filling with people preparing for bed. The train began to move. For two more hours she held on and we were almost there when it happened. She writhed and kicked, bumping her head on the underside of the upper berth, falling against the window, clutching the sheets, tearing at her clothes. She dug her fingernails into my arm and into her own face. She bit her tongue and there was blood on her mouth, but she did not cry out. I ran to find a doctor, found no one. When I got back, she was gone and the sheet was red. Even in the dim light of the corridor, I saw the dark stains on the carpet. An elderly woman putting up her hair in curlers gave a little scream as I entered the ladies' lounge. The toilet door was unlocked and there I found her. She could not hold up her head but the pain was less. A thick cord twisted down from her body through the toilet, out into the night and the wind and the clacking wheels below. I cut it with a razor blade, tied the stump with a shoelace. She fell as I knelt to help her up. The train had reached our destination, the conductor was calling all aboard. I just managed to get her off. She lay on a bench while I telephoned for help, but the doctor said he couldn't get mixed up in anything like that. Then she beckoned to me, said she wanted to go home.

Her parents were asleep and she got in unobserved. I walked about her house till morning, watching her window, telephoned throughout the day. Always she said she was fine, did not want me to visit. On the second day she met me in the park—pale, pale, pale.

VII

WIFE

MARRIAGE, TWO CHILDREN, Mark and Vicki; Topeka, merciless sun, the streets melt in August; years; Stockbridge, Massachusetts, the crimson woods, the deep snows, the Austen Riggs Center, psychoanalytic training; years; divorce. A second wife, another child, Joan, San Francisco, the far edge. A new life.

AFTER BREAKFAST ON a Sunday morning, Ilse prepared a picnic lunch and we set out for the beach. "Drive out Jackson Street," she said. "There's something I want to show you." Near the Presidio, she asked me to stop. We got out. "Look," she said, pointing across the street. Before us rose a stone promontory surmounted by a small château. The gray stucco of the building was but an extension of the promontory, an imperceptible transition. The stone dropped away sharply to the east; from below rose tall trees the tops of which embraced the house.

The front of the house was squared off, but through the foliage farther back could be glimpsed a circular structure, a red-tile roof, casement windows. The treetops swayed in the wind. We looked up to where the sun filtered through a Monterey cypress, glinted on the red tile. The front of the promontory was in deep shadow. The entrance seemed to be carved out of granite, winding into the stone, disappearing, emerging higher up, disappearing again, coming out finally near the top at an iron gate. The neighborhood was quiet; there was a faint sound of running water.

We were about to go on—I was opening the car door for her—when we heard a muted clang. I looked back up at the house. The iron gate was opening, several people moving about. The gate opened wide. Men in black suits were carrying something heavy; the sun glinted on brass fittings, a casket. "Oh!" a sharp intake of breath, she fumbled for my hand. I scanned the street; not far away, parked under a tree, was a hearse. "Let's go," Ilse whispered.

A woman with gray hair followed the casket. The six men moved slowly, with difficulty. The casket disappeared into the stone, reappeared lower down, disappeared again, finally emerged on the street. Ilse got back into the car; I watched from the sidewalk. The casket was put into the hearse, the doors were closed, the hearse drove slowly away. The woman reentered the passageway, disappearing and reappearing as she mounted the stairs. The iron gate closed behind her, this time with a distant, resigned clang. Birds sang, sun filtered through the cypress, sparkled on the red tile, again a ripple of running water, a breeze swayed the tops of the high trees. All was as it had been. I got back into the car, drove to Baker Beach.

Ilse put her arm through mine, pulled me out of a stroll into a stride. We walked near the high-water line of the breaking surf. She tried to tease me into a zigzag game of following after the receding waves, then running away from the pursuing waves, but I was not in the mood. She took off her shoes, ran ahead of me, the white foam swirling around her knees. We walked west perhaps a mile to where the beach ended on sheer cliffs, sat on a sheltered rock above the water.

"What are you thinking?" she asked.

"Nothing."

"I can't reach you. You're off somewhere alone."

She shook my arm when I did not respond, pulled me close, kissed my cheek. "Don't be in a mood. Come back to me. It's such a beautiful day. There's so much to enjoy."

We drove across the bridge, climbed the Marin headlands, sat in a high meadow, tall grass and lupines waving in the breeze, ate the lunch she had prepared, drank the wine. Whatever I said had a quality of making conversation; I could hear it. Gradually her spirits fell, and after a while she stopped trying.

Below us to the right the Golden Gate opened out into the Pacific, the Farallon Islands sharply etched on the horizon, to the left the bay with its thousands of white sails, Angel Island, Alcatraz, the far shore. Lines of strain settled around her eyes, minute beads of perspiration stood out on her upper lip.

"You just can't forget it, can you?"

"What?"

"The casket . . . A shadow falls for one moment across a beautiful day; you seize upon the shadow, will not see the sunshine. Why do you do that?"

We drove back to the city, to Fisherman's Wharf. Looked through a Swedish furniture store. At Ghirardelli Square we went upstairs for coffee, sat outside on a deck at a small round table by the railing. Below us in the plaza throngs of people

milled about in the waning sunshine. In a cleared area near
the fountain, ringed with spectators, a juggler was doing his
act. We were tired, looked at each other warily.

"Nothing works today," she said. "We get it together, briefly,
but it won't stay; it falls down. You keep thinking of that casket. That's what brings it down. I feel your thoughts lingering
on it, inquiring into it, caressing it; you want to pry it open, get
into it. I can't fight that sort of thing. You're sabotaging us."
She became more emphatic, her eyes angry. "You're obsessed
with death."

I felt sorry for her, wanted to make things better, put my
hand over her hands, looked out over the bay with its sailboats,
wondered how to comfort her. Her hands lay inert under my
hand. There is nothing holy any more. I remember the street
vendor, the mischievous grin, the heavy knife, and know that
my life is adrift in the same fortuity in which that hapless bird
lived and died, and know, further, that I must in whatever time
is left to me try to carve out some meaning from the all-engulf-
ing randomness.

I became aware suddenly of her eyes, wide with wonder and
reproach. Minutes had passed. She had withdrawn her hands.
"You're not even listening to me," she said. "You have forgotten I exist."

"ALLEN?" THERE WAS something hesitant in her voice on the
phone. "You remember the house I showed you, where we saw
the casket? It's for sale . . . Are you superstitious? I'd love to
see it."

The entrance at street level was through a Roman arch of
gray cement. We entered, turned right, went up one flight,
arrived at a heavily barred blue door. There the passage
opened, sky and trees appearing above us, the stairs doubled
back, then up another flight, this time in the midst of cypress
branches. A stone bench at a turn in the stairs. We sat on a

marble slab, looking through the branches around us, above the houses across the street, to the bay with its sails, the orange towers of the bridge, to Belvedere and Tiburon, and the brown hills of Marin.

Presently we climbed the remaining steps, in the open now, an iron railing at the edge of the cliff, the trees changing to pine and poplar, to an iron gate which stood open. This was where the casket had appeared. Beyond the gate the stone was level, a small plateau, the house on one side, an iron railing at the cliff edge on the other. Everywhere were flowers in redwood boxes. To the rear the stone dropped down, was replaced by soil, a small backyard, birch trees, magnolia, more pine trees, and a purple plum. The street was far below, the sounds of traffic distant and muted; the immediate sounds were the rustle of poplar leaves, the faint swish of pine, the trickle of water. Ilse pressed my arm, leaned against me.

Everything had been removed from the house. Dust stood in the corners. A few people wandered about. The rooms were few but large, plaster walls with panels formed by fluted moldings, plaster ceilings crossed with walnut beams, a circular dining room, and above it a circular bedroom. A tiny elevator ran the full height of the building. Beneath the basement level were two caves in the rock, the lower of which opened onto the stone stairway through the barred blue door.

The most elaborate room was on the top floor. A library with walnut shelves and walls, carved beams in the ceiling, wide casement windows above the tops of the surrounding trees. With treetops swaying below us on two sides, the bay to the north, the city to the east, we felt cut loose. It was an ivory tower, a sanctuary in the sky.

"Oh, Allen, we should buy this house. It's perfect for us. Our patients could enter that lower door, the blue door, and just inside we could make a waiting room. They could come up by elevator and leave by elevator; office and home in the same building would be entirely separate. What do you think?"

In this house we would never be far apart. "It fits you," I said, "better than it fits me."

"Yes! Yes! But if we lived here, maybe you and the house would grow on each other."

WE BOUGHT THE house. Ilse arranged everything, let her own work lapse, supervised movers, workmen, bought furniture, curtains. She was following a vision, moved dreamlike through the rooms, divining ways to make the house even more beautiful. She looked through many stores, decorator warehouses, auctions, before she bought anything, then would watch over its installation. And if, as happened occasionally, it was not right, she would send it back. The lower cave became a den, with Chinese carpets, lamps, shoji screens, Dürer prints, illuminated pages from medieval manuscripts.

"Are you happy here?" I asked. "I'm happy when we are together," she said.

At ten in the evenings I would come out of my study; we would talk, eat fruit and drink tea, go to bed. With the lights off, I loved to pull the curtains and open the casement windows; luminous sky would enter the room, would reproduce on white walls in sharp-edged blackness the leaves of poplar, the needles of pine. Soundlessly the shadows would rush back and forth. I would become drowsy watching them, Ilse's dark hair on the pillow beside me, her breath in my ear, while to and fro the shadows raced, paused, swayed, returned, and presently the room itself would become a cradle in the treetops, the old lullaby would come back, consciousness would slide a bit, that warm presence beside me, again that slipping of consciousness, and I would know that the next time it would slide away altogether. And if I die before I wake . . .

Are they together often?

AFTER SOME MONTHS the house was in order; the necessary
furnishings had been bought and arranged, and rearranged.
In the evenings Ilse was restless. Herself a psychoanalyst, she
had a gift for intimacy, and when the day's work was done
wanted only to be with me, while I, hurting still from an
ancient wound, was driven to search for a meaning that would
heal that wound and annul my father's accusation.

I would hardly be settled into my evening of work when
there would come a tapping at my door. Ilse would be suggesting that we go for a walk, or to a movie, or to visit a friend,
or would say she was lonesome, wanted to talk. I would lay
aside my work, but at such times my words were few. "You
want me to go away," she would say reproachfully. "You're just
waiting for me to be finished and gone. I can tell." And sadly
she would leave, and I would try to get back to work, but the
workshop of my mind would then be cluttered, and when
finally I managed to sweep clear the scraps of guilt, just about
then would come another tapping.

This time she would be more contrite and less forbearing.
"You're *making* me feel guilty!" she would cry. "I haven't done
anything!" And much sooner would come the moment when
she would say, "You want me to go, I can tell. All right! I'm
going. See if I care!" and she would slam the door. And when
yet a third time she had knocked and entered, had had her
presence suffered and again been dismissed, the whole house
would rock as she hurled shut the heavy door.

After some months I moved my work to the cave above the
waiting room. I was further removed now, but still she came
seeking me out. I would hear, from far above, the elevator door
open and close, the hum of the motor as she descended, then
the tapping at the door. Finally I locked the door, and when
she knocked said curtly, "Busy!" whereupon she hit the door
with her fist, cried out in pain, retreated bitterly. Then her
pride was injured and she knocked no more. After dinner

when I left her she would watch with large reproachful eyes, and when at ten I would come back she would be sad, and sometimes the dark blue eyes would be swollen.

VULNERABILITY DEEPENS AS I grow older. The slightest vicissitude is a laceration of spirit. A falling leaf opens a door on dread. I must beware. All things on this earth are coated with adhesive. Don't touch a thing; you'll become a collector. The briefest glance may lead to a fatal embrace. Involvements protect against dread, but dread is my subject and I must live it.

I am obsessed with death; and this obsession, I am convinced, is not a private terror but the unchanging rock wall to the stage of our existence. We block it from view with contrived sets of involvement, and though we know them to be fake, we labor endlessly to make them real. And as we go about those actions on that stage which accord with those sets, we come finally to believe they *are* real. The dark rock wall behind them is forgotten.

It occurs to me now that this metaphor gives me the two essential categories I need. One is that unchanging final wall. That is to say, the raw nature of existence, unadorned, unmediated, overwhelming us with dread. What should that be called? Perhaps simply the way things are. The other is that changing succession of stage sets which we put up in front of that wall, blocking it from view. What should they be called? They are the schemes of things, the systems of meanings, within which we live. The rock wall is a constant, too ugly and too fearful to be endured; the sets change over the course of history, though they may seem fixed over the course of a lifetime. The set, as in a play, is the arrangement in which we live, the scheme of things.

AT NIGHT, WORKING in this dungeon room, this prison cell of books, I hear, faintly, from upstairs, music. Waltzes, Edith Piaf, Kurt Weill. And occasionally I hear the sound of feet, a rhythmic swish, and I realize suddenly she isn't walking, she's dancing. By herself! She has soft breasts, blue eyes, and a passionate nature, a face always ready and hoping for love and laughter.

WE ARE SPENDING the summer in a vastness of dark forest, impassable brambles, sunlit coves, broad beaches of cream-colored sand. An island in Puget Sound. Ilse found it, an old farmhouse with an outlying cabin which serves as my study. Joan, my younger daughter, loves it. Within minutes she had discovered dozens of living creatures. Monty, her dog, walks along the beach wagging his tail, waiting for someone to throw something. If no one obliges, he wanders missionless into the water, explores the rocks with his paws, puts his head under the water to pick up a shell, comes up a dark dripping gold, sometimes a strand of seaweed across his nose.

Here I work in the open air, on the porch of the cabin. I sit in an old wicker rocking chair, my feet up on another chair, sur-rounded by books and papers. The air is cool, the sky overcast, the Sound gleams silver through a filigree of leaves. The chip-munk chatters in the Douglas fir. I feel, in the midst of these tall trees, an exhilarating lightness. An old neglected apple orchard slopes away to the beach. Water laps at the shore, gulls scream, the blue heron stalks fish, lifting his spindly legs one after another in long, cautious advances. There is a brooding northern remoteness here that suits my task.

IN THE MORNINGS while I work on the porch of my study, Ilse works in the house. She pulls down the gaudy wallpaper, pink flamingos in tropical marshes, covers the walls with burlap, makes curtains for the windows, shelves for the kitchen. After a few weeks she becomes restless. "I'm too much alone," she says. "I'm bored. Tell me what you're writing."

"It's too complicated."

"You just don't want to bother."

"No. It's difficult."

"You mean I wouldn't understand it?"

"I can't talk about work in progress."

"Let me read it, then."

"Later, perhaps."

"You don't think I'm smart enough!"

"You would understand it, all right, but you wouldn't like it. It would upset you, and you'd want to talk about it, and that would upset me and then I wouldn't be able to go on."

SWALLOWS HAVE BUILT a nest under the roof of my porch a few feet from where I sit. With all the other places available to them—house, barn, shed, water tower, the whole unpeopled island—they choose the one place I have chosen for my work. And that would be all right with me—I would share quarters with a mother swallow—but it's not all right with her. It makes her nervous for me to be so close. She wants me to leave. Moreover, she has a husband and a lot of friends. All of them are after me. They circle and scold and, one after another, bank and swoop on me as dive-bombers on a battleship, pulling up at the last moment. "That nest has got to go," I say. Joan is shocked, disbelieving. "You wouldn't tear down a nest, Daddy! Not with eggs in it!"

My concentration is lost for the morning. I go for a walk on the beach, thinking I will take it down when she is occupied with other things. In the afternoon, returning to my porch, I find a sheet of lined paper pinned to the rocking chair. On it, printed awkwardly in crayon:

Dear Sir,

I know you have work to do, but I'm going to have babies. Please don't tear down my nest.

Sincerely,

Bird.

I PICK UP my gear and move inside the cabin, surrendering the porch to the swallows.

JOAN'S BIRTHDAY. ELEVEN years old. Many presents. A bicycle basket from the island of Madeira, a tepee, a birdhouse, a hammock, which I have strung up between two apple trees. Ilse cooks a beautiful cake.

The next day I am back at work. I sit in my study, a two-room cabin, very old, made partly of logs, roofed with hand-split shakes. At some distance is the house, similarly old; to the left the down-sloping orchard ending in a blackberry patch, then a wide stretch of beach, the steely blue water, and in the distance the snow-covered Olympic Mountains. To the right, solitary, is Mount Rainier. A strong wind today and a roaring sound in the high trees—fir, cedar, maple, madrone, hemlock.

Outside my window, Joan rides her bicycle with the new basket. She is just learning, pushes hard on the pedals, rides around and around in large circles, Monty trotting along with her. Her face shows intense concentration. She does not see me, does not know that I watch. Her hair is drawn back and held in a clasp at the back of her neck. She wears a new magenta blouse with blue-tape collar and epaulettes. Fair face, clear profile. Sometimes it surprises me how much I, who expected only to look after her, have come to love her. *4.5*
daughter

THE EGGS HAVE hatched: the nest is ringed with wide-open red mouths rimmed with yellow. There is a constant coming and going of swallows bringing worms. Not just the mother and father; the uncles and aunts are pitching in, too. The nest is too small, and one of the nestlings fell out. Joan picked it up, cradled it in her hands. Standing on a chair, I reintroduced it into the nest. The next day it fell again. Again I returned it to the nest. Joan put a mattress under the nest in case it continued to fall. On the third day it was clear the parent birds were pushing it out. "We should not put it back any more," I said. "They won't accept it."

"What will become of him?"

The tiny creature was no bigger than my thumb. Not yet a fledgling, only the prickly beginnings of feathers. Eyes still closed, the only indication of life a quiver of heartbeat. At the time it had first fallen, it would open its mouth when it heard the chirp of swallows; now it did not respond. "It's too little," I told her, "it won't survive."

"But what will become of him?"

"There's nothing can be done."

She looked down at the filmy bit of life. "We can't just let him die," she said.

She built a nest of straw in a box, covered the straw with flannel, put the nestling in it, put the box in the kitchen near the stove. Every hour she would pry open the tiny mouth and introduce a drop of warm milk and honey. Sometimes the bird would seem to ingest it; most of the time it would drain away. This procedure took all of her time; she hardly paused to feed herself. The next day the bird was still alive, even opened its mouth. "Look, Daddy, he's better!" She was radiant.

It didn't last. The third day it was weaker, could not respond. I began to help her; the two of us spent the whole day trying to get nourishment into a thimble of barely living tissue. The fourth day it died.

Her mood was somber. "We should have been able to save him," she said. "He was so little. All of his life was still to come."

She buried him in the orchard. The next day I chanced upon the tiny plot. A cedar shake, gray with age, had been pushed into the ground. On it the single word "Bird."

THE PROBLEM IS: How grasp the world? How take hold without dislodging someone else? And should we care?

I LIE ON soft earth, looking up into a clear night, into the eye of that vast spangled disk, whirling around its dark center trailing arms of frozen fire. I am looking into endless night. The spin grows faster. I am taken with vertigo. My fingers spread, I seize the grass, try to force myself back into the earth, that I not fly away. My wife, beside me, is calm.

No moon. To our right the feathery blackness of tall Douglas fir, to our left low, round trees, ghostly white. Above us a cloudless black velvet sky, sequined, glittering, minute pulses of red, green, blue, and gold; remote, icy. Beneath us the soft loam of the orchard.

"I feel the earth," she says, "its tremendous size and weight, the slow turning . . . and, sometimes, I think I can feel the even slower movement around the sun."

Why is it, I wonder, that she is part of the world, while I stand outside trying to grasp the world? Perhaps because she trusts it and I don't. I try to stop the turning, she goes with it.

A mild night. Windless. The trees are still.

"Once," she says, "I thought that if I exercised my eyes, if I practiced hard, I could make them very strong. Then I would be able to see a great distance, maybe a mile . . . How far can one see?"

"As far as light can travel," I say.

"Farther," she says. She raises an arm, points. "See that black space? Sight sinks in there . . . goes on forever."

A faint breeze moves across our faces. Apple blossoms fall, alight like snowflakes in her dark hair. *Like snowflakes:* with words, I try to grasp the world.

"The world has become very large," she says.

"Oh, look!" she cries, then points. I see nothing but night sky, stars. "It's moving. There! Bright. Must still be sunlight up there." I look harder, see nothing. "It grows faint, then bright. See! Now faint . . . now bright. It moves. It's tumbling . . . slowly . . . over and over . . . like a barrel."

She sees better than I, and farther. I aim my gaze along her upstretched arm, and presently among the fixed stars make out the star that moves.

THAT WAS SPUTNIK. A great leap in power. The world stood in awe, jaws agape, squinting heavenward for a glimpse, some faint metallic glint, of the tiny moon we had hurled into the sky, becoming thereby meddlers in the celestial mechanics of which previously we had been but observers. Newspapers carried a diagram to explain this latest marvel: a tower projecting from a spherical earth, a man atop the tower throwing a rock that falls in a steep curve, returning to earth a short distance away. A more sophisticated but still Stone Age man with a slingshot throws his rock farther, the arc of fall more gradual; at Crécy, a longbowman achieves a much greater reach; gunpowder hurls a projectile thirty miles; and now rocketry imparts such a thrust that the force that would have our missile fly away into the void equals the pull of the earth that would bring it down. Equi-poised between these forces, it hangs there like the moon, circling over us, effortlessly, forever—as the earth moves around the sun, as the sun circles the dark eye of the galaxy, as the galaxy itself spirals perhaps about some primal and final black hole.

NOTHING STAYS. PRESENTLY, being able, we throw our rock even harder. It moves in a widening orbit, drifts away.

We too are drifting away. We struggle to hold the world in our grasp, but without our knowing we fall away. What is this world we're always wanting, always trying to grasp, always losing?

In the beginning the world is the womb. We are fully and tightly enclosed, tied by a gnarled rope. There follows that most violent expulsion, shock and terror, slash of cord, and the world is lost. And found again. The world is the breast.

Bleeding cord is consoled at flowing nipple; we latch on with mouth, dig in with fingers. Presently the world enlarges, includes now a face bending over, a smile, a lullaby, the sound of footsteps. The world is mother. The fingers relax; the world slips away a bit, becomes larger.

The world now is father, brother, sister, aunt, porridge, orange juice, bowel movement; the world becomes family, home, Christmas tree; becomes school and bicycle and skiing, and a girl with dark hair and smiling eyes; becomes ambition, visions of the future, children of our own; becomes automobiles, airplanes, trips to distant countries, history, world affairs, the threat of war. The world slips away, we're falling outward, but the view becomes ever more grand. Shining and bright, like a blue jewel, the world spins there before us, seemingly within our grasp, while we, like a satellite weather station in widening orbit, camera pointed steadily earthward, see the world with increasing comprehension, but remain unaware of the void behind us into which we are falling.

THE GREATEST ENLARGEMENT of world takes place in adolescence. Centrifugal force increases, we are hurled away. The family that had been so large a part of our world, indeed all of the foreground, recedes, shrinks, all but disappears. We fall back, fall away. The world is vast, enlarging, while we are shrinking, our life diminishing. "We are a phantom flare of grieved desire," wrote Thomas Wolfe, "a ghostling and phosphoric flicker of immortal time." In my teens, in the thirties, finding myself so small a part of something suddenly so vast, this abruptly deepened perspective on the world found its definition, its most perfect expression, in the novels of Wolfe, in those trains of his hurtling through the night across those vast plains.

As this world view took shape, I felt myself entering upon maturity, coming to grips with the world, approaching something like mastery—like Gide in his garret, late at night, pen poised above paper, looking out over the snow-covered roofs of a sleeping Paris, saying, "Now you and I will come to terms." I didn't know that I had fallen *away* from the world, that this new and exciting view was a function of greater distance, relative to a continuing fall, hence no more final than those it had replaced. It seemed, rather, that in the past I had seen the world through the colored glass of a child but that now, having reached a stable orbit, I saw it as it is, the way things are, the real thing, and that this view, therefore, though it would be further clarified and refined, need never be superseded.

Years pass, years of unnoticed fall, and one day, in the fifties, reading Salinger, or perhaps the early stories of Updike, I begin thinking of Wolfe and realize I haven't heard much about him in recent years, and I look back at the page before me and realize suddenly that the world has changed, that that vision which had seemed so final has been replaced. A different world is portrayed here, different not in the sense that individual differences of style and temperament make for unique vision—the works of Hemingway, Wolfe, and Faulkner being instantly distinguishable one from another—but different in the sense that the world addressed in common, although in their several distinctive ways, by Hemingway, Wolfe, and Faulkner, is most certainly not the world of Henry James and, likewise, is not the world of Salinger and Updike.

Now it is the nineties and Salinger is gone, and Updike a senior citizen, and one day, reading Rezzori or Kundera or Gombrowicz, I find once again that the world has changed.

I'm falling, falling, and the farther I fall, the faster, and it's long been clear that no view is final, that all of us are falling, that senses fail, vision dims, sound is muffled, and all that is left of that too solid earth and its cloud-capped towers is that ephemeral blue dream reeling away in the void.

TALL, SILENT TREES and the cold northern light, the long trailing evenings with the sawtooth Olympics cutting blackly into the darkening sky. Joan sits in the sand and dreams away the end of the day. An exhausted and contented Monty lies motionless at her feet, gold fur sticky with salt. Ilse broods. I observe. Joan is happy, belongs here as do the swallows coming back every year, the deer nibbling in the orchard, the chipmunk racing over the roof at night.

ILSE AND I sit at a table in the sun. We have finished lunch, are having coffee. We are at the edge of a cliff, look over miles of blue water to a wooded peninsula and another island, above which Mount Rainier rises abruptly from the sea, solitary, covered with a glimmering whiteness merging with the blue-white sky. Ilse wears an orange halter dress and a straw hat. Through the filigree brim of the hat the sun makes a bright grid on her cheek. Her brown arms rest on the table.

"There's no place for me here," she says. "I'm not needed. Except as a cook. I don't mind cooking if I'm also a companion, but I won't be just a cook. Joan can fix your meals. Maybe you'll like that better . . . You don't *want* a companion. You don't speak. Whatever you think, whatever you feel, it stays inside. You don't tell *me*. After breakfast you disappear into that study and talk to God. Joan wanders off into the woods and talks to animals. I have no one to talk to. I wait."

Monty comes racing up to the table, pushes at my arm. I look up. Down the slope in the orchard Joan is on her knees, hair falling over her face. Presently she stands, lifts her cupped hands to eye level, slowly opens them. A movement of head indicates her observation of a ladybug in flight. I shift the coffee cup as Monty paws at my arm.

"I'm not important to you," Ilse says. "You care about Joan and you care about your work. That's all. I'm like Monty. I keep nudging but can't get your attention. He wants to tell you something. And you look up. But as soon as you reassure your-self that Joan is all right, you lose interest. But it's still impor-tant to him. Maybe he's found a snake and wants to show you."

She stands. "Come on, Monty. *I'll* go with you." She holds out her hand and starts off, but Monty won't follow. He sits beside me. "*Nobody* here wants me," she says. "That's why I'm leaving."

I draw her down beside me, put my arms around her, kiss her. "*I* want you. What does it take to convince you? Have you forgotten last night?"

"Last night! Ha! Why is there nothing left over? Why are you not *with* me? *Really* with me?"

"Remember how cold it was at midnight? How we wan-dered through the orchard, arms around each other? That blackness of forest, that icy blaze of stars? And later, how warm?"

"And where is it now? Where has it gone? All morning you were in your study. On the cross! Why do you leave me alone? Always! Always! I would take you down and bathe your feet, but you'll have none of it. You want the nails left in place. You don't believe you could stand up on your own, move around in life and just *live*. You *bequeath* your life to posterity because you're afraid to *live* it with me. Your passion goes into your work. Your romantic feelings go to Joan. I get what's left, the carnality. Thanks a lot! Even that could be something. I try to make it mean more to you, to spill over into the rest of living, to mean to you what it means to me. I can't *tell* you. I try to *show* you. Something in you holds back."

In the cold night she flings herself wide, takes me in beyond her control of what may at such depths then happen to her. I am touched by her trust and by that response which wells up in her, gushes over in a voice from another world. "Oh, Allen! . . . Allen! . . . Darling!" By allowing me to touch her so deeply, she makes me a god. Her arms are tight around me. I am the source and the object of her passion. It begins and ends in me. The world has disappeared.

But my desire does not end in her. I reach into her for something that lies beyond. My heart is a galloping hoofbeat, but in the dark press I pursue a secret end. I strain into her for something to carry me away. Not the wave that lifts us both; something else. Something I reach for but do not touch. I just miss. And when the wave drops me back in the same bed alongside the same woman, who sighs in utter happiness and snuggles against me, and I caress the soft black hair and murmur in her ear—then under cover of darkness failure pools in my eyes. I have been close but have missed.

I hear the hum of eternity. I think of the trolley at the foot of Nob Hill, cable thrumming under the street; I'm the gripman, I lean back on the grip, the car hooks on, begins to move, is carried up, up, to the top. Such a strand is running here, silently, powerfully. I feel its presence, close, somewhere in this darkness. She and I are but momentary thickenings on this endless strand. Our grip is failing, we are falling away, the cable slips by us, through us, faster, faster. Straining into her I seek the silken strand, want to seize it, be carried up out of this valley of death.

"I feel used," she says.

A HIGH PLATEAU in western Washington. A country road. Around us for miles and miles are level fields of wheat. "Look, Daddy!" Joan is pointing. "The wind is making rivers in the wheat." I stop the car. We get out, stand by the fence. Monty runs about happily. It is midday, bright sunshine. A cool gusty wind blows our hair, makes a rushing in our ears, a whispering at our feet where the wheat bends and sways. Monty finds a patch of deep grass, rolls over on his back, growls, twists, turns, paws the air. The wind pushes us from behind, and the streaming forward of Joan's hair is continued unbroken in the swath of bending wheat that begins before us and sweeps out in long curving arcs. In the vast field we see, here and there, many such rivers and streams. In the far distance the Cascade Range rises up first green, then blue, then gray, to a jagged snow-covered crest. There is no car, no person, no sound but the cool rushing wind and the whispering wheat. The grain is heavy, ready for harvest.

The atmosphere is peculiarly light and bright. A feeling of exhilaration comes over me. Joan looks at me and smiles. She feels it, too. The wind covers her face with a veil of hair through which I see the blue of her eyes. She laughs, and the veil spreads over her mouth. She is wearing a velour shirt the color of the field before us. Her eyebrows, I notice, are heavier, darker. The swell of her breasts rises, falls, with her breathing. I see in her still much of the child, but the woman is coming on fast. With my finger I trace curving strokes in the pile of her shirt. She acknowledges with a smile my analogy to the wheat. The wind rises and the field before us swarms with currents. "The fingers of the wind," I say.

Again we are pushed from behind as by a giant hand, propelled forward. The thrust carries on in the wheat at our feet, writhes, twists, sweeps away. Monty, taking the commotion as evidence of an animal, leaps the fence and disappears in pursuit. The wheat is well over his head but we follow his course by the disturbance he creates. He leaps this way and that as the wind suggests an elusive, darting quarry. Presently, as if realizing he has lost not only his quarry but also his bearings, he stops to think or to listen. Then he barks.

Joan and I, realizing at the same moment that he is asking for help, call his name. He hears but mistakes our whereabouts, rushes off in the wrong direction. We call again. He seems confused, perhaps by the rustling and whispering. He veers, circles, backtracks, goes farther afield. Again he stops to listen. Again he barks, now with a note of distress. The wind

rises. It's not possible now to know which of the many currents of disturbance is Monty. He yelps, sounds farther away.

"Daddy! He's lost!"

She climbs through the fence. I follow, take her hand, hesitate. I don't want to trample this ripe grain, but there seems
no choice. "You stay here and try to see where he goes," I say.
From somewhere in the field, Monty howls.

"Wait!" Joan puts a hand on my arm, utters a long, clear
call: "MONTY! JUMP!" And jump he does, his head and
back clearing the grain. "JUMP!" And again he jumps. And
again. And now he has the sense of it: as he comes into the
clear, his head turns in quick purposeful search. Now he sees
us and comes swimming toward us, disappearing under the
golden sea, emerging like a dolphin in long sweeping arc, his
ears at the top of his leap standing out horizontal, disappearing again, swimming under water, faster and faster, leaping
again, exultation on his fur face as he gets closer and closer.
And now he is upon us, home! and leaps straight up in the air
before us, and licks our faces.

JOAN'S SENSE OF the sanctity of life seems to be a conviction
not that she has arrived at but that she was born with. Not an
ideal but a fact, the way things are. And not only is all life
sacred to her, but—with a simplicity and certainty that seem to
place it beyond question—equally sacred. She does not refrain
from value judgments, as between her life and Monty's life; it
seems, rather, not to occur to her that lives might be ranked in
importance.

HAVE BEEN SITTING in my office in total silence. Have tried
to read several books. Can't read. Desolation. Am removed
from my task. The few lines I write in my journal are my only
tie with life, with significance, with creative effort. Notes in a
bottle.

Utter quiet. Nothing to distract me from the silence within, or from the silence toward which I am tending. The task to which I have for so many years felt myself called is to create a vision of life in its largest and deepest perspective. Have lost contact with that goal. I grope for it but can't seem to touch it. Am unable to work, missionless, feel useless, empty.

Have been talking to myself. "Wait. All is vanity. What you write or don't write makes no difference. Don't drive yourself. Wait till something of importance impels you to expression." But can't rest. The trouble is that it is just this making of something that itself claims importance, independently of the importance of its content.

JOAN IS TOURING Canada with her high school class. Monty has taken me as his master, follows me around as, when she is here, he follows her. As we walk through the woods of the Presidio, he runs ahead, sniffing here and there, often goes some distance away, but checks frequently on where I am. If he loses me, he comes looking at the place I would be had I continued at the same pace in the same direction as when last he saw me. He never has any difficulty. His mood as we walk along is exploratory. He's looking for something. He pushes his way through bushes, always sniffing. There is about him an aura of eagerness and excitement, as if at any moment some great thing may happen. If then I bend over and pick up a stick, he is instantly before me. The great thing has now happened. He has a mission.

Head raised, nose pointing the stick, one foreleg motionless in midair, tail extended, he is transformed. Nothing remains of that friendly, tail-wagging creature who sidles up wanting to be petted. Nothing remains of Joan's companion, of the games, the indolence, the random spontaneity. All is gone. Nothing remains of affection. There is a hard, glinty look in his eyes. They do not attend to me; they are fixed on the stick.

He has become an essence of poised readiness, of total dedication. Everything else in life—food, dogs, scents, play—everything, has fallen away. Even I, his master, have fallen away, am nothing now but the holder of the stick, which it has become his mission to retrieve.

And if, still holding aloft the stick, I try with my free hand to pet him, he ignores the gesture; his eyes do not soften. If I persist, he will avoid my hand with an impatient jerk of his head. His task has been assigned, he is ready, he awaits the throw. I throw the stick and he is after it instantly. Were I to have thrown it over an abyss, he would have leapt after it. He plunges into the high, crashing surf of the ocean with the same unthinking dedication as into a placid pool. It never occurs to him to evaluate the mission. His dedication is solely to its fulfillment. He runs or swims any distance, over or through or around any obstacle, to get that stick.

And having got it, he brings it back; for his mission is not simply to get it but to return it. Yet as he approaches me, he moves more slowly. He wants to give it to me and so bring closure to his task, yet he hates to have done with his mission, to be again in the position of waiting. For while *I* hold the stick, there is nothing he can do but wait. It requires my throw to release that great energy. Curious, while I hold the stick, though I am of no importance to him as one whom he loves, I am absolutely essential as the source of his mission. He cannot make his own assignment, cannot throw his own stick. He can hide a ball and then find it, but that's a game, whereas this is the meaning of life. The fixed, somewhat fierce passion of his gaze and his readiness to give his all attest its importance.

For him as for me, it is necessary to be in the service of something beyond the self. Until I am ready, he must wait. He is lucky to have me to throw his stick. I am waiting for God to throw mine. Have been waiting a long time. Who knows when, if ever, He will again turn his attention to me, hand out my assignment, and allow me, as I allow Monty, my mood of mission?

I SIT HERE listening to Mahler's Ninth Symphony. Has been six months since my last bit of writing. Seems as if I have nothing to say. Work with patients seems vaguely fraudulent, insubstantial. Am remote from my task. No vision is near, no aura. I may be mistaken, it may come tomorrow, but my intuition is that it is far away. Cannot conceive what it will be. It's not around the next corner. Many turns, many silent streets, wet, dark, menacing, before it and I meet.

I have mistakenly entered one of life's off-ramps. There before me is the red warning: "Stop. Turn back. You are going the wrong way." But there is no room to turn around, and I am, anyway, propelled forward by an invincible momentum.

Strong wind in the cypress tree. Foghorns in the distance.

"YOU'RE IN A trance," Ilse says. "Are you looking for those hidden threads . . . still?" I smile, nod. "Well, don't! Come, sit down. Pay attention to me. It's bad enough you leave me alone all week. Don't leave me while you're still here. The weekend isn't over yet."

I sit on the bed, the dusk of the room thickening and flickering. She takes my hand. Her fingers are feverish. "Tell me," she says, "what could be more important than our being together?" "I have to work." "But what? What is it? What really do you do?" The fingers of her hand are unsatisfied, wait, continue to ask. "You're a psychoanalyst," she says. "You know already a great deal. Why isn't that enough?" I make a deprecating gesture. "I want to find the pattern that . . . falls away in the night."

The air seems to become milky. Fog stands at the window. The sounds from the street are muffled. The faint reflections of red have disappeared.

"YOU HAVE A terrible mind," she says. "It takes everything apart. So what can you find? There's nothing there. Of course! Because you've taken it apart! Life is in the configuration of things, the relatedness. You can take a watch apart and put it back together and maybe it will still tick, but you can't do that with a flower or a kitten—or with me. That's the trouble with you. You're a mechanic, but life is not a machine.

"I'm different. I try to make people *see.* A face, a flower, a dog. Particularly a face in the moment of a changing mood, a flower turning toward the sun, a dog hearing a strange sound. I say to people, 'Look! This is life. Isn't it marvelous! Isn't it wonderful!' But you don't do that. You look at the world and you see what I see, but you pay no attention to it. You're not interested in the surface of life, only in its depth. You ignore the face and surmise about the bloody psychodynamics.

"And as for the flower, that's just a nuisance for you, something to be watered. If it weren't for me, there'd not be a single plant in this house—or around the house—because they require attention and so keep you from your precious work. And the same for the dog; if it weren't for Joan twisting your arm, there'd never be a dog in this house. You're not interested in faces and flowers and dogs. That's life, but you're not interested in life itself, only in understanding life. So you hardly glance at life, you're in such a terrible hurry to *understand* it, to master its causality, the theory, the principle, how it works.

Life threatens you, so you want to control it. But it *can't* be controlled. That's its nature. Once you can control it, it's gone. And if ever you finish your theory, get everything worked out, you'll find yourself king of the dead. Nothing will stir in your realm. Not a breath of air."

ALL MARRIAGES ARE quarrelsome and difficult, all except those good marriages that are good because one of the pair is passive, allowing the other to dominate, and, since rights are respected only to the degree one is prepared to defend them, eventually to demean and to exploit, whereupon over time the compliant one accumulates submerged rancor so massive, expressed in the modes of that same passivity that once expressed the love, that the marriage fills to the rooftop with coldness, until finally beneath the facade of harmony there is nothing but a block of ice.

Do not dwell on the shortcomings of your marriage, or on the unfortunate personality traits of your wife. Dwell rather on what is right about it, what is fortunate, what is blessed. Do not feel deprived because of what you have not, but fortunate because of the great deal you have. When things become abrasive, try to focus on how *you* (I'm talking to myself) can make things better by being more adroit, more empathic, more sensitive.

For *all* marriages are unhappy. None of my friends and none of my patients has a happy marriage. An unhappy marriage is the normal state, not a deviation. The unfortunate reaction, therefore, is to feel bitter about it, to nurture a grievance, to imagine that married to someone else one *would* be happy; for this reaction leads one into actions and attitudes that make an unhappy marriage *more* unhappy, rather than into those responses which would tend to make an unhappy marriage *less* unhappy.

The main reason for misery in your marriage (I'm still talking to myself) is your tendency to think that you're entitled to a happy marriage, that with a little luck you would have had it. You must accept the given unhappiness as normal, and proceed immediately to do whatever you can to diminish that unhappiness. What you have is the human lot.

But don't expect much. And remember: there is no occasion for grievance.

That rare, rare thing, a happy marriage, is a mutual capitulation, an agreed-upon diminishment of life. The once lovers agree to be blind to what they have lost. They live in a cloned closeness to escape an anguished separateness, do not permit themselves, even in the privacy of their own minds, to harbor views or values unacceptable to the other.

THE OPPORTUNITY TO love is ever present. No one, in his loneliness, need ever say, "I wish I had someone to love." That someone is right there. The trouble is she has become real, while only the still imaginary inspire us to love.

ILSE LOVES TO travel, to walk about in strange cities, breathe a foreign air, hear another tongue. Swimming delights her; the presumptuous intimacy of the unresisting medium makes her laugh. She likes to talk with friends, always wants to know what they are doing, to hear about their children. She loves to walk, to feel the sun on her face, to browse in new stores, to visit museums and look reverently upon the past.

All these things, so desirable to her, I find tedious. She does not, however, like to do them alone; so I go along, and while apparently participating, actually am waiting for whatever it is we are doing to be done with. And as I go on like this, tolerating in benign martyrdom a way of life created from her initiative, it comes somehow to seem that, on my own, I could arrange things better, that I *know* how to live, but am constrained by her needs to banal diversions.

One day something goes wrong with my knee. I'm not so crippled as I portray, but enough to be excused from obligations. My wife is all sympathy, tells me it will get better. "What do you want to do?" she says. "Come! Get in the car. I'll drive. It's a marvelous day. We'll go anywhere you want, do anything you like. It's Sunday, it's springtime, the sun is shining. You mustn't be sad. Where do you want to go?"

I have no idea. Anywhere. Nowhere. My mind is not blank, but neutral. Places parade before imagination and all are

Futile! Oh, so close to home?!

equal. She drives us to the beach, thousands of people swimming, oiling themselves on bright towels, playing in the sand; along a golf course where we pause to watch a man take three practice swings, then hit a perfect drive, the ball sailing straight away, up, up, and out of sight; by a museum with a show of French Impressionists, throngs of people entering and leaving. In the park we drive by picnickers, teenagers throwing Frisbees, barefoot girls playing volleyball, young couples pushing baby carriages, smells of cooking, of charcoal fires, sounds of baseball, of guitars, and of laughter. My wife, delighted with this panorama, drives slowly, glances at me eagerly, ready to stop wherever my inclination may suggest, do anything I want, go on to any place I wish, while I, looking out on this unhesitating life process, fall into a well.

Every one of these people *knows* what to do, how to enjoy it. It looks terribly simple, yet I have not the knack. I can *do* these things, go through the motions, simulate the responses—to an observer it might seem that I, too, know how to enjoy a holiday—but in the manner of a brain-damaged patient who, thinking intently what each leg must do, can somehow get there, yet not with a natural walk. I lack a kind of native knowing which is the legacy of everything that lives. Now, suddenly, without the *obligation* to do those many things which, as it seemed, I have been *bound* to do, I have nothing better to put in their place, indeed, nothing whatever to put in their place. Free, I cannot improvise. Relieved of my burden, I am bereft.

How strange! I have worked hard all week, now along comes a day of utter leisure. Must there not be something I want, something that would give me pleasure? I must observe these people more closely. There must be a secret, some simple solution.

Always and forever the student and still I don't know how. Are there no classes in living? Would someone take me on as an apprentice?

NOT KNOWING HOW to live is separateness, the division of the world into self and others. I sit inside my skull and look out as a frightened man from a moated castle. Me in here and the world out there. We negotiate, we make deals, exchanges, but we are not one. I am an entity, complete. Never do I lose sight of where I stop and the world begins. With sleepless vigilance I patrol the edges of selfhood, warn visitors away. I am independent within this domain, but am dying. It is my wholeness that destroys me. I long for partness in a greater whole.

Knowing how to live is oneness with the world. I die of the hunger of oneness. I find it never. I read about it, and the words are ghosts. Dharma is not for me, nor "the way" of Lao Tzu. I feel it in the patience of trees, the wind in their branches sighs about it. I hear it in the rote of the surf and the song of the lark. I see it in animals and in children. I touch it but cannot make it mine. *Mine!* I'm trying to grab it, I suppose, ravage it back into this moated castle, and that's the trouble— this division of everything into self and others which I can't escape because it's not something that limits me, it *is* me. I stand on a ledge.

WE ARE HELD in life by commitments, as broken bone by a plaster cast. "The man who desisted from committing suicide because he heard the factory whistle blow," writes C. E. Ayres, "was thereby recognizing a profound truth, namely, that his existence is so intertwined with those of other people that his death must inevitably send forth waves of disturbance and interruption, affecting most those who are closest to him but also prejudicing, to however tiny an extent, the whole effort of mankind."

I have severed relations with the factory, the whistle blows but not for me. I cling to nonattachment even as I suffer from it. For so long has it been my way that, however wrong in principle, it has become for me right. I owe it loyalty. It has come to be the source of all that I can do. Desperate unrest is my workshop.

"None but the truths which have been extracted under mental torture appeal to us," writes Cyril Connolly.

ILSE HUNGERS FOR intimacy as cut flowers for water, cannot make peace with my sense of mission. Suddenly, as we walk, her hand pushes its way into mine like a tiny frightened animal seeking shelter. "I've been thinking," she says, "over and over—it's such a trite thought—we've lived together so long . . . then one day one of us will die, and . . . will never see the other any more." She lives in others, ascribes nothing worthy of immortality to the isolated self even if that self be her own.

How brief and fitful our time.

I DO NOT use myself up in living. A part of myself I save, like a miser, hoping to transmute it into something that will go on living for me in the future. With the quick I have little to do; the eminent dead are my models, the yet unborn my legatees. I am a time-binder, obsessed with mortality, spend my life creating an effigy to outlast me. In the graveyard, ceaselessly I carve at my epitaph, trying to make of it something so beautiful, so compact of meaning, that people will come from afar to read.

It need not be in vain, this elaboration of self—great treasures have been so fashioned. What gets served up to the future may be a tasty dish indeed, but what shall we say of the chef, oblivious of the hungry ones around him, garnishing himself for the gourmets of the future? Rather than miss a day of painting, Cézanne did not attend his mother's funeral. Rilke could not spare from his poetry the time for his daughter's wedding. The world cannot do without such people, but pity those whose lot it is to live with them.

I think rather more of those who use themselves up, die

with nothing left over, disappear without a trace. My wife holds nothing back, spends her life on the living, gives herself to the hungry, who feed on her, consume her substance. I see her getting smaller, becoming transparent, beginning to disappear. But look at her face! It grows finer, more beautiful! She has time: Come and be fed. She prepares no delicacies for the future, but soup today for everyone, even for those hungry chefs who think only of posthumous banquets. Better get to know her now, for she will soon be gone, and you'll not then recover her from the history of our time. But without the likes of her, there would be no future for which the present could be a history.

I FIND MYSELF wanting to fall in love again. With her of the volatile spirit, the open and generous heart. I have been holding myself aloof for years, invulnerable, to protect the search. But love can't live on the shelf, must be fed with those confidences which create vulnerability. Without risk of hurt, there is no love. Not, anyway, of the kind we used to have, she and I—the soaring, the despair, the exaltation.

Now I have no search to protect, have lost direction, find nothing, create nothing, want back the deep, deep joy. I must open myself to pain, must see it as minor beside the passion it makes possible.

"WHY DON'T YOU talk to me?" Ilse says. "What are you preoccupied with?"

"My work."

"Why can't you be preoccupied with me?"

"With you I'm more than preoccupied. I adore you."

"I don't believe it. What are you writing?"

"I can't say."

"Why not?"

"It'll go away."

"Is it fiction or nonfiction?"

"I can't talk about it."

"Is it about me?"

"Listen, Ilse, I'll tell you a story."

"It's about time!"

"A few days ago I was walking in a dark wood. A heavy mist, like a white sea, lay about me. From it rose the black glistening trunks of tall cypress. There was not a sound; my footfalls were noiseless in the soft turf. Overhead the green canopy was lost in white. I walked slowly, the heavy dampness suspended around me, began to feel a mystery in the whiteness. Then a strange thing happened. I saw a bird. It was sitting on a low branch. I could not see it clearly because of the mist, but well enough to realize it was of great beauty, of such brilliant plumage as never before had been seen. A deep happiness came over me. Never had I encountered such a lovely thing. I felt a great longing to show it to others, to everybody . . . "

"Everybody but me!"

"No, you first of all, and most of all. Then to everybody. But I couldn't move. I hardly dared even breathe. I locked my gaze on the eyes of this shy, wonderful creature, knowing that at the slightest move or sound it would fly away, and that then neither I nor you nor anyone would ever see it again.

"But I knew—no, rather, I hoped, I believed, and still believe!—that if only I observe it steadily enough, with enough devotion, and in purity of heart, eventually it will come closer . . . and then closer . . . and closer . . . and as it approaches, I will see it more and more clearly, and finally it will alight on my hand, and this wild, wonderful thing will have become tame. And then, you know what I'll do?"

"I can hardly bear the suspense."

"Ilse! What will I do?"

"You'll call your publisher."

"No. I'll call, 'Ilse! Ilse! Come see what I've found!' And you'll come. You'll be enthralled. And then I'll want everyone else to come, too."

Her eyes are wet. She is weeping, through her anger, for all the lost years.

Beauty of this moment & grief over all the times he avoided these moments w/her.

VIII

THE ARCHITECT

THE PIGEON WAS interfering with his work, his livelihood. The vendor got angry. Why do you make such a thing of it?

Because . . . if he had whacked off the head . . . in anger . . . sure. I could accept that. But the feet!

Head, feet, one pigeon more or less? What's the big deal?

There's a lot in life that can only be mourned; there are some few things that must be hated.

FROM 1934 TILL 1953, my mother lived in Marion, Louisiana, in the big house where she was born—tower rooms and light-ning rods, curving verandas, filigree gingerbread, porch swings, and a vast yard with massive oak trees and towering sweetgum trees, all surrounded by a white picket fence.

When Oliver grew too old to practice medicine, he still went every day to his office in the store, sat behind the dusty rolltop desk with the skull and the scales and the microscope, and talked with customers and visitors. He became in time a nuisance for Kleber, who wanted him out of the way. "You've lived long enough, Papa," Kleber would say. "It's time for you to die." Oliver would view him warily: "I'm better acquainted around here, son, than I will be anyplace I'm likely to go. So I reckon I'll just stay awhile longer."

In 1935 Molly died, and a year later Oliver. My mother stayed on then with her brother Kleber and his wife and daughters, and with her youngest brother, Clayton. On Sunday mornings she taught Sunday School and stayed for the sermon at the Methodist church, Tuesday evenings she went to choir practice, Wednesdays to prayer meeting, and every morning she walked up the red clay road to the school on the hill where she taught third grade. I visited her in Marion once or twice a year; and, whenever invited, she would visit me—in New York or Topeka or Stockbridge, Massachusetts.

IN 1946, BACK from the war in the Pacific, I had just begun psychiatric training at the Menninger Clinic when my mother again fell sick. After a few weeks her brother, my uncle Kleber, telephoned from Marion to say that she was hospitalized in Monroe. When I spoke to her physician on the phone, he could tell me nothing except that she was seriously ill, diarrhea again the main symptom; perhaps a salmonella infection. Nothing could be cultured from her blood or her stools.

When I arrived at her bedside, I found her extremely weak. She was running a fever of 102 to 103 and had developed phlebitis of the left leg. Her hemoglobin was low, presumably because of the continuing bowel hemorrhage. "It's a nonspecific ulcerative colitis," her doctor said. "There's nothing to be done but bedrest." I discharged the doctor, transferred her to another hospital, and found a good internist.

I lay on a stretcher beside her bed as blood was taken from my vein and dripped into hers. She improved a bit. All lab tests were still negative. I thought she had an intestinal parasite and undertook to look for it, still close enough to my medical school days, I hoped, to recognize something like an amoeba. I spent hours in the hospital lab examining stool specimens under the microscope. And found nothing. And was about to give up when one day, searching among the myriad of vegetable cells that characterized every slide, it occurred to me that these were not vegetable cells at all but *Balantidium coli*, a large protozoan. And a pathogen. I had been seeing these cells for days without recognizing what they were.

I rushed to the atlas of parasites to verify my discovery; the internist and the lab director soon confirmed it. It was a runaway case of balantidiasis. She was started immediately on Carbarsone. Her temperature dropped to normal on the second day; her appetite returned, she was able to eat; and by the fourth day the diarrhea and bleeding were over.

This experience completed her apotheosis of me. "If you had been my doctor thirteen years ago," she said, "I'd still have my teeth." To anyone who would listen, she extolled my virtues, my accomplishments, and as she grew older her praise became excessive, eventually fatuous. "He saved my life. Not just once, twice! I would not be here today except for him. He is a *supreme* diagnostician! You can *mark that down!* The doctors had all given up. They didn't know what to do. They could *not* make a diagnosis. They didn't know what medicine to give me. Then *he* came. He was engaged in very important work in Topeka, Kansas. In *psychiatric* work. At the Menninger Clinic. But he dropped everything. He laid it all aside and came to see about me. And when he arrived—well, that's when everything changed. He got me the best doctor, and put me in the best hospital. He gave me two pints of his own blood. That's what *really* cured me! And then he made a diagnosis. Nobody else

could do it. They all tried. They couldn't do it. He looked
through the microscope, and kept looking, and kept looking,
until he discovered the cause. And then he knew what would
cure it. Carbarsone."

In her family, in childhood, she had learned that men bear
the weight of the world; women are helpmates. Only men may
hold authority, deserve admiration; women tend to be foolish,
weak, and easily frightened. Now she pushed this invidious
stance to a further extreme, disparaged her own intelligence
the further to exalt mine. "Let me tell you . . . what was wrong
with me . . . it was so rare, so difficult to diagnose . . . that I
can't even pronounce it. What is it, Allen? Balytodisus? Baly-ti-
dai-pus? You see? I can't even say it!"

Her recovery was not, however, complete. The phlebitis left
her with a permanently swollen foot and leg. The ankle had
disappeared; the leg was now of uniform size from calf to foot.
A special shoe was required. She walked with a shuffle. Over
the years, whenever she came to visit, she would ask me to go
shopping with her for elastic hose. And always I would go, but
in vain. The hose that she was able to pull on did not provide
enough support, while the hose that did provide enough support was impossible for her, with her fumbling ways, to pull
on over the swollen foot.

WHENEVER SHE VISITS us, a change comes over my wife: she
becomes abrupt, almost curt. A reaction, she says, to my mother's overly fond behavior with me. I understand; I, too, am
often embarrassed by my mother's need to be near me, to
touch me. When, before retiring, I go into the kitchen for a
snack, my mother will always follow. "Can I get you some
milk?" she will say, though the answer is always no. And
always she will kiss me good night, holding me a few
moments longer than I would wish.

On summer evenings after dinner, the three of us will sit

outside. When night comes, my wife will go in, and then my mother will begin to reminisce, her voice taking on a tone of clandestine warmth and intimacy. When I, too, wish to go in, she will lean toward me in the darkness and take my hand and say, "Don't leave me, son, not yet."

WHEN IT CAME time for her to retire, she wanted to leave Marion, to settle down near one of her children. Where should that be? She wanted to be near me, but I advised otherwise. I would probably be leaving Stockbridge soon, I told her, I didn't know when or where, and then would doubtless move still again. She should not tie herself to my uncertainties.

My advice was like an order. Disappointed but obedient, she turned to my sister, bought a little house in Midland, Texas, one block from June.

But was not happy. She did not complain to me, but complained a lot to June. To me, she was respectful, admiring, deferential, tactful; to her daughter, she was dissatisfied, demanding, often scornful, sometimes contemptuous. June had married "beneath her station"; Francis, her husband, "lacked breeding and culture," he had "no refinement, no education"; both were subjected to relentless comparisons with me. She was constantly telling my sister what to do, what to stop doing, how to live.

And Francis himself was demeaning of June, putting her down, spraying her with sarcastic cracks. Caught between the two of them, my sister began to falter. She was able to survive only by virtue of her work; for she was a much-loved schoolteacher, becoming eventually superintendent of schools, and this vocational success was ballast against the buffetings at home. But when forced by age to retire, she was rendered helpless. Francis too was now retired, could devote himself full time to the put-down of his wife; and my sister, subject now to hammer blows from both quarters, began to fall apart.

INCREASINGLY IT SEEMED to me that I was the architect of my mother's life, and as the years passed—straining and adventurous for me, gray and impoverished for her, years of waiting, always waiting for my rare and brief visits—it seemed that I unintentionally had designed for her a barren life, and that she was obediently following my blueprint, unable to break away from my spell, and I powerless to free her.

So perhaps my dying father was right to fear that she would fall for the first man to lay hand on her flank, but he could hardly have known that that man would be me, that therefore the promise not to remarry which he extracted from her could not protect her.

Futile

THE LITTLE BOY

Why are you haunted by that pigeon without feet? That Flying Dutchman of the air?

I was there. I looked into those twinkling eyes. I have been made custodian.

Is not the pigeon an odious bird? Are we not blessed when there is one less? However dispatched?

No. Not "however."

But do you not know about life? The way things are? That the great men of history are great because of sending others to die? Their greatness proportional to the numbers slaughtered?

I do not accept the way things are. I abhor great men.

Then why not mourn something worthy? At the Falaise Gap, the Germans fell so thickly that, afterwards, for hundreds of yards you stepped on bodies, on limbs, viscera, heads—all of them sons and lovers, all webbed in hope, drenched, each one of them, in memory and desire. At Tarawa, the U.S. Marines clawed their way ashore on and over and through their dying comrades, amid their screams, their hands so bloody they could not hold their rifles. At Bergen-Belsen, the naked Jews, white and stiff in death, bounce like firewood as they are thrown up on the roof-high stacks. And you—you are upset about a pigeon?

No act of cruelty must go undespised.

Was not that vendor a man like any other? Is there not cruelty in all of us? Did not that vendor go home, like the rest of us, and dandle his granddaughter on his knee, comfort her when she stubbed her toe?

He may dandle her on his knee till hell freezes over and still I'll hate him for what he did to that bird. I will never forget, will never forgive.

A FEW DAYS after my mother comes to visit, usually as we sit at dinner, she turns to me. "Son—" she says, her tone and manner announcing something portentous, "son, I'd like for you to show me your office." As if she had never seen it before—though in fact she sees it every time. And a day or two later, "Don't forget . . . I'd like you to show me your office." Not that she wants to *see* it; she wants *me* to *show* it to her. "All right," I say, "let's do it right now."

We squeeze into the tiny elevator, descend, I open the double doors, we enter my private realm. Teak parquet floor, teak-paneled walls, rosewood bookshelves to the ceiling, Oriental rugs. A deep silence inhabits this room. It embraces her, enfolds her. She smiles, begins a slow tour, touches the spines of books feeling a vast awe at what I have read, examines the pictures, is contentedly bewildered at the Expressionist prints, content because their incomprehensibility to her is tribute to my sophistication and acumen; examines the couch. "Do your patients lie here?" "Some of them." She lies down. "And they talk?" "Yes." She sits before me in the large chair of brown leather.

"What do you *need?*" she asks. She wants to make something for me to use in this room. A pillow for my couch perhaps; she has saved some pretty silk scraps, could put together a very nice pillow for me, she'd love to do it. Or perhaps a lap robe for my legs on cold days; she would crochet it in dark blue mohair. Or something else. Anything.

I sit directly before her in my own massive black leather chair. In silence, we confront each other—son to mother, psychoanalyst to patient, Oedipus to Jocasta. She strokes the soft leather, caresses it. "Your patient sits here?" "Yes." "Where I am sitting?" "Yes." "And you sit there . . . where you're sitting?" "Yes." "And she . . . your patient . . . talks about herself—is that right?" "Yes." "And tells you all her troubles?" "Yes." "And you tell her what to do?" "Well, not exactly."

She falls silent; a look of vast longing spreads over her face. *She* wants to be my patient, wants to come every day, and not just for fifty minutes but for a session without end, wants to tell me her troubles, all she longs for.

But she does not permit herself to say these things. Watching her face, I see the exact moment her thoughts veer away from unutterable longing to a less anguished realm. "So she sits here and talks, and you sit there and listen? . . . Is that right?" "Yes." She clicks her tongue slightly. "Son—" She lowers her voice, and something of incredulity, perhaps of faint reproach, and yet of pride, enters her voice; perhaps she remembers the life of her husband, my father, as a country doctor. "Son, you have a *mighty* easy profession."

AND ONE MORE time, often on the eve of her departure, she will say, "I'd like to see your office once more—before I go." And again we fit ourselves into the tiny elevator and descend, and again she walks around my room, touching things, looking, thinking. In the upper rooms of this house I belong to my family, and she is a visitor; but here I belong to no one. This is the realm of my private self. Here she encounters only me—me, for whom she is searching. She thinks of what she might make for me that I would use in this room. She wants to create something with her own hands, with love, that will stay here with me always, her surrogate, always with me.

IN 1970, WHEN she was eighty-one years old, a mass appeared in her right breast. Over the phone the surgeon said it was cancer, recommended radical resection. I demurred, decided on a simple mastectomy if it were confirmed as malignant.

When I arrived in Midland, she was so happy to see me that she forgot about the operation. When reminded of it, she wanted me to examine her.

"That's not necessary, Mama."

"But I *want* you to feel it."

"No matter what I might find," I said, "you would still have to have the biopsy."

"I know, I know, but I want you to feel it."

"If it *is* cancer, Mother, we're concerned that it not spread. So the less manipulation the better."

"You're my doctor," she said. "Your hands couldn't hurt me."

She took off her blouse, took off her bra, stood directly before me. "Lift your arms," I said. I could see a slight puckering of skin in the upper outer quadrant of the right breast. When I took the breast in my hands, I found the mass to be about the size of a golf ball, irregular in shape, very hard.

"The biopsy will be done while you're anesthetized," I told her. "You must be prepared for the possibility that when you wake, your breast will have been removed."

"I'm prepared," she said. "I'll do whatever you say."

So the breast was amputated. There were no metastases. She recovered quickly.

"I'm still your mother," she said—proudly, defiantly— "even with just one breast!"

WHENEVER I INVITE her to visit, she instantly and happily accepts. She comes several times each year, stays two or three weeks each time. After ten days or so I will see a worried expression, she will touch my arm, say, "Well," very tentatively, "I guess we should think about my getting back home." A bleak little trial balloon; she's hoping I will shoot it down. And I do: "It's too early to think about that. You've just got here." "Well . . . " The tension drains away, she sighs, a contented look comes to her face, perhaps even something of smugness, of possession.

She is outspoken and fulsome in her praise of my wife, but the ulterior aim behind these ostensibly spontaneous outpourings, hidden from her, is painfully visible to the two psychoanalysts whom she so disingenuously addresses. My wife becomes irritable, I become uncomfortable.

After a few more days, "Well, I guess I should begin packing up now," she says. "I guess I've had my visit out." "Why don't you stay another week?" I say. "Well, son, if you're sure I won't be in the way." "You're not in the way at all." She seems content with these negotiations, perhaps even feels herself to have been deviously successful.

And now she has seven more days to be with me—a lifetime! Anything can happen in seven days.

But then the seven days are gone, and we are at the airport, the loss imminent and unavoidable, and what then is urgently present in her tremulous voice and gait, the tension in her fingers on my arm, the desperate searching in her eyes, is that she wants to stay with me forever, that no *visit* could ever be long enough, that any separation is a death.

DURING HER EIGHTIES, my mother's upper spine slowly collapsed, diminishing her height by about six inches. Her esophagus, now much too long for the shortened distance from her throat to her stomach, formed kinks, and the swallowing of solid food became difficult. A huge hump formed on her back.

At ninety she was deeply stooped over, walked with a cane in small, slow, shuffling steps, and what presented forward as she came toward me was not her face but the crown of her head. Her face stared at the ground; she had begun her final plunge into the earth. When she heard my voice and saw my feet before her, she would reach out and climb my arms with her hands, thereby managing to lift her face enough to see me.

When she was eighty-three it had become evident that she could not continue to live alone. She was doddering and indecisive in street intersections, got lost on the way to the grocery store. I persuaded her to enter a nearby retirement home where several of her friends now lived. At ninety, she became incontinent, had to be diapered, needed assistance in dressing and undressing and in bathing; so I moved her to a nursing home. She was no longer steady enough to walk with a cane; she got about the hallways slowly in a walker. In the short distance from her room to the dining room, she would lose her way.

ALWAYS I DELAY calling her—because it is so hard to get off the phone. One thing reminds her of another; the chain of reminiscence is endless, ranges not only over her own long life, but gathers in friends and relatives, extends back into what her grandmother told her about her great-great-grandmother. That's the way it was until her ninety-seventh year when, one day, I realized with surprise that I had called her during my ten-minute break between patients, that I had fallen into the habit of calling at such times, and that it was easy to get off the phone. The stickiness was gone. Her densely peopled past had, like old film, faded to uniform gray.

When I go to visit her in the nursing home, I try to bring it back. "Do you remember our house in San Antonio?" She looks puzzled, then troubled, "No, I can't say I do . . . not exactly, no." I then describe it for her, the kitchen, the long veranda, the hackberry tree, the mesquite, the honeysuckle that covered the fence, the cot on the back porch where I slept. As I talk, I see in her face glimmers of recognition; I step up my pace, try to compact those glimmers into a chain reaction of recall. Everything is lost. I ask about her marriage. Nothing. Her years in college? Nothing. I remind her of the time when her father took her as a little girl on a riverboat to New Orleans, where, having bought an entire bunch of bananas, he locked her in the hotel room so she would be safe while he went off to play poker. The high point of her childhood. I've heard it a hundred times. Don't you remember? Nothing. She peers back into a void.

Young black women, enormous, slow-moving, strong, lift her off the bed into the wheelchair, onto the toilet, wipe her behind, bathe her, dry her, hold her up, dress her. She watches, helpless, troubled, as they ransack her drawers; things once carefully folded tumble about under heedless, uncaring hands as they search for underwear, nightgowns, hairbrush, dentures, blouses. She does not trust these women. She hides the candy I bring her in bottom drawers, inside vases, behind photographs.

She has misplaced her pearls. I search her handbags, her desk, her closet. Going through the pockets of her clothes, I come upon a piece of dry cake wrapped in Kleenex, half an apple, gray with age. Under a pile of stockings I find a carefully wrapped sandwich. "That's for the little boy," she says. But no pearls.

As she lost the past, she lost also the present. Vision blurred and dimmed; she could not read or write, could not make out what was happening on the television screen. Books and newspapers fell away. She no longer hears the telephone: I must call the nurses' station, ask that someone go to her room and pick it up for her. No more does she shuffle down the hallway in a walker; she lives in a wheelchair.

Emptied of past, bereft of present, without future, she begins to create an imaginary world. "The little boy has been hanging around today," she says. "I think he wants to talk to me, but he won't come close. I'm gonna get some candy; he'll like that."

Over the months this little boy becomes a companion, a fixture in her life. She worries about him. Where are his parents? They should be looking after him. A little boy like that needs a home. He should not be out alone at night. She would take him in herself if she could, but it's hard for her to get about. Always she tries to feed him. In the dining room she asks the waitress to set a place for him. "Ain't no little boy here, Miz Wheelis," the waitress says. Whereupon my mother becomes cross, demands an additional plate, and, not getting it, puts aside some of her own food and takes it back to her room.

SHE LOOKS AT her hands. Ancient, withered, discolored, gnarled with arthritis, leaping veins and tendons. A plain wedding band on her fourth finger, a large amethyst in gold setting on her middle finger. She touches the rings, hesitates, moves them back and forth, finally takes them off. "Look at them," she says. Her manner is portentous. Inside the wedding band: OMT and MBW, June 19, 1908. "I want you to take them with you . . . to keep them safe." I protest: She enjoys them, she should keep them. "No. I'll lose them. You take care of them for me. Keep them safe. I want Joan to have them . . . someday." I drop them into my pocket. Her eyes follow their disappearance, linger on the pocket.

On my next visit, as we sit talking, she seems to be waiting for something. "Where are my rings?" she says. "In San Francisco, Mother. Don't you remember? You wanted me to look after them for you . . . so they wouldn't get lost." "Yes, but I could wear them while you're here. They'd be safe as long as you're with me." "Well, that's true," I say, "and I'm sorry I didn't think of it myself. Next time I'll bring them."

A few months later I'm back, and give her the rings. She receives them eagerly, hungrily; with something like a sigh, a visible relaxation, she slips them on her fingers, she is whole again. During the next two days, I watch her affirm herself in these rings. They contain the past that is lost to her. When it is time for me to go, she again, reluctantly, surrenders them. "No, Mother, I'm not going to take them. They would simply lie in my desk. Useless. But you really enjoy them. I want you to have them. I want you to wear them all the time."

THE VISIT IS over. "Good-bye, Mama."

She fixes me with a look of solemn entreaty. "Son"— she takes my hand, presses it between both her own—"son, why don't you take me back with you? I wouldn't be much trouble and I could help with the chores."

I look at the sagging eyelids, the clouded, unseeing eyes. Incontinent, unable to feed herself, strapped in a wheelchair that she not pitch forward. "I'd like to, Mama . . . but you're too weak to make the trip. You have to get back some strength first. Then I'll take you."

She looks at me dubiously, takes a grain of hope, but not more. It flickers briefly and fades. She stares at the wall, then turns to me in desperate resolve. "Well, I can tell you one thing," she says emphatically, "if you ever get down bad sick and have to be hospitalized, then I'm gonna come out there and look after you. I'm gonna come . . . even if I have to walk every step of the way. I'm gonna see to it that you get the *prop-*

er medical care, and the *proper* food to help you get strong . . . and then I'm gonna stay a while."

ONE DAY, HAVING neglected her for a while, I call the nurse to get my mother on the line. There comes the thin, vacant voice, changing to warm as she recognizes me. She wants to talk but has nothing to say. I chat, I tell her news of my children. She doesn't remember them. I describe them to her, relate her experiences with them, try to make them come back. Nothing. She does not remember that I live in California or she in Texas, does not know what month it is, what year. She reproaches herself for having neglected her parents recently: I tell her they have been dead for fifty years, and that she was a great comfort to them in their last illnesses. She is reassured. And when am I coming to see her? She thinks I am just around the corner, cannot imagine me two thousand miles away.

"And how is the little boy?" I ask. "Oh, he's all right . . . I reckon." "Do you talk to him?" "Oh yes, I talk to him." "And does he answer you?" "He shies away. Don't seem to want much to do with me." "What's his name?" I have never asked this before. "Why, his name is . . . Allen"—slow wonderment spreads out in her voice—"Wheelis. . . ." A slight startle of breath, a double take. "Funny." She hesitates. "He has the same name as you."

Silence. I wait. Will she discover significance here or only coincidence? The moment drags, passes. Nothing. My childhood is lost to her. "Sometimes I won't see him for quite a spell," she says, "but then one day I'll hear a blood-curdling yell." She chuckles. "And then I'll know he's around."

That cry leaps from a deep well, without context or connection. She has no idea what it means, nor why she feels comfort rather than alarm. But I know. I remember that cry and the fantastic power it claimed.

THE LITTLE BOY   189

AT TWELVE I discovered Tarzan and fashioned an identity on the life of this dauntless and unvanquishable savage. I would live in the jungle as he did, would survive on but my own strength and ingenuity, would be protector of all the friendly animals and the terror of the evil ones. I took Tarzan as my middle name. The trees roundabout were carved with the letters ATW. I wanted to depart civilization at once but knew I was too young. I had to wait . . . to prepare myself. But how long? Until sixteen, I decided. Then I would be ready. But would my mother let me go? I must get her promise.

I held close the details, said only that I wanted to live in Africa. "But at sixteen? No. You have to go to college." "Please, Mama." "We don't have to decide now," she suggested. "You're only twelve." "Please, Mama. It's terribly important to me. Promise." "I can't promise such a thing, son. It might not be right for you. Let's wait." "I can't wait, Mama. I have to know now. *Please!*" She is silent, troubled. "A lot can happen between now and then," I add deviously, encouraging her to believe that I will change my mind about wanting to do such a thing, that therefore she will never have to deliver on this promise; while knowing that I will hold her to it even though I, in bad faith, seduced her into making it. "Just say yes. Please, Mama!" She sighs. "All right, hon."

The way is clear, the fantasy unrolls. At sixteen, I will hitch-hike to Galveston, get a job on a freighter. Eventually this freighter will touch at Casablanca, where I will jump ship, find work on a coastal steamer going south. At the mouth of the Congo I'll pick up a riverboat, go upstream, deep into the interior. The river narrows. One night I will silently let myself over the side into the dark water, swim to the shore, disappear into the trackless jungle.

I viewed the next four years as preparation. I must become strong, must acquire the basic skills of survival. I raced down the veranda, leapt to the mesquite tree, swung about on the branches. I practiced climbing with ropes, threw spears, made flint knives. And frequently, after mortal combat, I rehearsed that celebrated moment of epiphany: Placing my right foot on the body of vanquished foe, I threw back my head, beat upon my chest, and uttered the victory cry of the bull ape. I had never heard such a cry, nor was I, in Texas, likely to. Knowing only that on hearing it all the "denizens of the jungle" trembled, I improvised the loudest, most prolonged and alarming cry I could imagine, then practiced to make it uniform, distinctive, and terrifying.

And one afternoon, lost in my reverie, forgetting that my mother was entertaining the ladies of the Bible Society, I placed my foot on the body of Numa the lion and uttered my cry. And the ladies leapt to their feet, teacups flying, faces blanched at the murder evidently taking place in the next room. But my mother was tranquil and reassuring. "Oh, that's all right," she said. "Pay it no mind. That's just Allen . . . practicing."

MY SISTER DEVELOPS Alzheimer's disease. Gradually her memory slips away. After a few years she knows nothing, can no longer feed herself. Francis puts her in the nursing home alongside my mother. Neither recognizes the other. My sister wanders the hallways, smiles benignly, but does not speak. Francis dies of cancer; she knows nothing. She comes upon her mother, stops and stares at her with fixed and uncomprehending smile. My mother glares. "What is that woman doing here?" she cries angrily. "What does she want? Why is she staring at me? I don't like that! Something ought to be done about a situation like this. Where is the management? I'm going to report her!"

A TELEPHONE CALL from the nursing home. "Your mother is crawling around on the floor. We can't think what's got into her. Never been like this before. We pick her up, tie her in her chair, but first chance she gets she'll slip right out, sorta slide down, and then there she'll be, crawling around again."

I ask the nurse to put her on the phone. After a while I hear the struggle, the labored breathing. "Hello, Mother. How are you?" Pause, then the thin, infinitely tired voice. "I guess I'm all right, son." I ask about the crawling. She begins to cry. "I've lost my rings."

The world is lost to her. Those rings were its vanishing point. When next I see her, she still slides down out of her chair, gropes about on the floor, but no longer knows what she seeks. Everything is slipping away. She still has a grasp of me, though at times she stares blankly as if I too were fading.

X

VOICES FROM THE COUCH

CONNED BY MY own inhibition. The sidewalk in front of the health food store. A bright, sunny day. A flushed man in a straw hat, chanting, "Stop the bomb! Stop the bomb!" hands me an antinuclear leaflet, holds out an oatmeal box with slotted top. "We must stop nuclear war," he says. "Help us out. Even if only a dollar."

Worthy cause. Cheerful man. I reach in my pocket for a dollar, start stuffing it into the box. At that moment three things happen simultaneously: (1) I see that I have taken a five-dollar bill by mistake; (2) he says, "Oh, God bless you, sir! You have *made* my day!"; (3) I realize he is a charlatan. My fingers still touch the bill, but the jubilation in his voice, perhaps in anticipation of the drink he will now buy, prevents me from withdrawing it. Having been identified by him as generous, I am ashamed to reveal myself as prudent. The transaction is over. He instantly closes up shop and hurries away.

NEUROSIS IS INHIBITION and anxiety. And what is normality? The freedom to love and to work. So we say. But is there not something disingenuous about this jaunty loftiness? What are we hiding? Normality is the free pursuit of power—curbed, in deference to prevailing morality, only enough to keep up appearances and to stay out of trouble.

SELF-AWARENESS COMES INTO being in the midst of struggles for power and is immediately put to use. One defends oneself or seeks advantage by misrepresenting oneself. One doesn't think about it; it happens instantly, automatically, inalienably. It is not possible to abstain. One cannot be oneself. To be human is to be false. Awareness is inseparable from misrepresentation. The soul of self-awareness is deception.

Revealing myself, I remain hidden. As the real self is exposed, it becomes false, the now real self retreating in shadow. Honesty cannot know itself; aware of telling the truth, I lie. The pure heart, blind to its own purity, sees only outward; the reflective heart is devious.

Unaware of weeping, I show you a moment of authentic grief; be quick, it's gone in a flash. As I feel the tears on my face, knowing how they may alter *your* reaction, grief is mediated, is being staged. "Say everything that comes to mind," the analyst says to the analysand; but the second association is a comment on the first, and the third watches the second, and the bottom of that barrel can never be scraped. Below the deepest uncovering one yet deeper is possible. Dirt is endless. Fur and feces and bones, and ever deeper, but no bedrock. Authenticity is fugitive in self-referential systems; awareness builds layer by layer while reality flees forward.

The first time I came here . . . I was pretty much mute, kept stumbling, didn't know what to say, how to ask for help, or for whatever it was I had come to get . . . and you said, very calmly, "Talk to me. Make me know what it's like to be you." That was strangely comforting. I could feel myself relax, I knew I was going to be known, and I trusted you, and I knew right then I mustn't hold anything back, that would be foolish, I had to tell you everything, even the worst—especially the worst—otherwise it would all be just a waste. So I realized, that very first day, there was no possibility of seducing you, no use even trying.

Which means, of course, that she *will* try, that seduction is her characteristic way of relating to a man, which means she suffers low self-esteem, which she tries to overcome by demonstrating sexual desirability, which means that the effort to seduce that she renounced on that first day will surface here again and again, unavoidably, the degraded self-image being hidden behind a mask of charm and sexiness, all this destined to evolve between us, foreseen now as a glimpse into the future, a future that, in turn, will gradually disclose a determining past.

You know what Camus said about this? "It is difficult to return to the places of one's early happiness. The young girls in the flower of their youth still laugh and chatter on the seashore, but he who watches them gradually loses his right to love them, just as those he has loved lose the power to be loved." That's elegant and elegiac, and true, but it is not my condition. My trouble is the loss, not of the right to love them, but of the ability to fuck them. No, that's not right either. It's the loss of the desire to love them, being left only with an itch to fuck them.

I'm ashamed, also angry and confused. What is this, anyway? Do you guys have an explanation? Is this an infantile conflict—to be analyzed? Or the way things are—to be accepted? Why this degradation of the sexual drive? I've had this longing all my life, but it used to be something quite different. It was always sexual, I think, and perhaps the union of bodies was always the culmination. But it was not carnal. In essence it was spiritual. Ethereal. The raw energy of sexual drive, like fuel for a rocket, was used for loftier purpose and was able thereby to lift the longing into a higher realm. I was concerned with symbols: the dropped handkerchief, the veiled face, the red rose, the scented stationery, the way the letter was signed, even the way the stamp was affixed. Where has all that gone? I used to idealize a beautiful face. Margaret Sullavan, those candid eyes sweeping over me so close, like a touch, soul to soul, that husky voice, that exalted courage in one so frail. It would choke me up. Those were the things that swarmed in my mind. The yearning was for love, for melting into one another. I would never have permitted a word like "fuck"—or "screw"—to associate itself with my desire, and I would have turned in fury upon anyone who suggested that that was all it amounted to. I wanted love, I wanted the two of us to become so precious one to another that a crisis calling for the sacrifice of life would come almost as a relief. A tragedy too, of course, since it meant a parting, but a relief in that it would enable me to prove in action what otherwise could only be professed: that I loved her more than life itself. Where has all that gone? That's what Camus talks about. Maybe he didn't live long enough to come upon the degradation of this yearning with age.

But Evan Connell did. This is how he puts it, the kind of girl he's looking for. "Abandoned. Lascivious. Dissolute. The more dissolute the better. Everything that I am not but would like so much to be. A young lady experienced in each conceivable depravity, totally intemperate, unbuttoned, debauched, gluttonous, uncorked, crapulous, self-indulgent, drunken, and preferably insatiable. Never mind if it is an adolescent dream, never mind. There may be no such woman this side of Singapore, but I won't settle for less." And he adds, "How different from the pains of youth. Here is no thought of pressed flowers, moonlit walks along the beach. Here is the meaning of the body's work, its need; the rest is wasted time." That's where I am.

When I see a beautiful face, an elegant aristocratic face, limpid eyes, delicate exquisite mouth, instantly I see that mouth sucking cock, my cock. Those virgin lips open, open wide, take in the engorged member, hold it hungrily, lasciviously, suck on it, while the cock plunges deeper and deeper into the slender, swan-like throat. And while the dreamlike face is thus engaged, anchored on my prong—no, not anchored, transfixed, impaled—the fawnlike eyes roll up to gaze at me gazing down on her. I want to see everything. The more light the better. Mirrors everywhere. I want to watch, to savor in minute detail, the disappearance of my cock into an orifice, any orifice, mouth, cunt, ass. Doesn't matter. The more the better. One after another in sequence.

Should one live long enough to imagine such things? Should not such a person be put to death for the good of society? Isn't there something apocalyptic in this? Something to destroy the world? Do you feel this way? Would you tell me? Is it perhaps my own death coming closer, closer?

What am I trying to do, anyway? What do I really want with such a girl? I don't want to hurt her, but it's very clear I'm not wanting to love her either. Maybe I want to disappear altogether up her cunt and enter her womb. Is that what I'm after? What makes this hunger so desperate, so anguished, so altogether insatiable?

On second thought, Camus did live long enough. He knew all this. He was dealing with the same thing, but euphemistically. He dressed it up, bathed it in Proustian nostalgia. That falsifies it. Because it's not elegant or elegiac or wistful. It's primitive and brutish, the spirit failing, falling back soiled and tattered and dirty, as the old animal sinks back into the earth.

Sometimes I'm filled with horror at what I am becoming, at what I already am. At a movie—one of those soft-porn leering teasers—I'll hear the laughter of a man behind me. Dirty, guttural, wet. The kind of laughter that revels in baseness, that finds its pleasure in the pulling down of spirit, the lower and the dirtier the better. And in that laughter I see myself. Not that I laugh; I am silent, chilled, appalled. I want to turn around, scowl, disavow any commonality with one so base. But I am there, the same as he, and that laughter draws my portrait as surely as it does his.

It is the common coin, the carnality in us all. But once I rose above it, used it to power a transcendent soaring. Out of sex I made love, out of flesh I made spirit. "Who knoweth the spirit of man that goeth upward, and the spirit of the beast that goeth downward to the earth?"

What has happened to me? Am I not the same man? Somewhere? In some lost corner of myself? Can you find it? Why cannot the ideals that shaped and guided that soaring lift me now? They seem empty, weightless. The wind of years blows them about. Husks in autumn. I feel deceived. I suspect them of being illusions, of having always been illusions. What I regret now is lost sexual opportunities. Only that. Only that makes my youth seem wasted. As death gets closer, only carnal pleasure seems real. It's brutish, it's dirty, it guarantees nothing, but it doesn't deceive.

So maybe I should simply accept the portrait of me drawn by the wet laughter in the dark movie house. Maybe that's all there is, all there ever was. Take it or leave it. That or nothing. Maybe I should climb down from my high horse and stop feeling superior, stop being offended, just slap my knee and roar and whoop it up with the rest of the dirty old men.

IN THE NEWSPAPER I come upon a new advertisement among the pornographic listings: Marguerite in the Afternoon.

It's refreshing in the morning, it's the bread of life at night, but have you tried it in the afternoon? With Marguerite?

The picture shows the upper part of a naked girl sitting in bed. Alone. Ornate bed, fancy room. Perhaps a bordello. Short blond hair, face soft and pliant. No evidence of character. Quite young; maybe seventeen. Features unfinished. Full lips, mouth slightly open, eyes averted, a dreamy look on her face. Perhaps masturbating. She is, I imagine, in her first awakening to passion. I feel the lust rise in my veins, in my mouth, can almost taste the free-running juices of this girl.

I shift the paper, the light falls at a different slant, and I find myself looking at my younger daughter as she was at about fifteen. What had been a rumpled sheet beside the prostitute appears now as Joan's Teddy bear. It jars me. Something flips. I am rushing to her rescue.

I tilt the newspaper, find I can alter the image at will. From one angle, the girl is a stranger, object of my lechery; from another, my daughter, claiming my protection. The shadow can be the rumpled sheet of abandon or the Teddy bear of innocence, as I will. Shifting the picture back and forth, I realize that what is jarring me is not the changing image before me, but the changing orientation within. Each shift of image occasions violently opposed intentions. I am not one person perceiving something out there in one way or another, but am one person or another person depending on what seems to be out there.

I position the paper to reflect my daughter, observe the inner configuration.

The girl is not an object of desire, is not an object at all. She is a person with a history, with memories, who had chicken pox while vacationing in Big Sur, who came sleepwalking into my bedroom after her first day at school, who had a terrible time with algebra, who would slip her hand into mine and ask me to help her, who still, to this day, gnaws at her fingers—a person dear to me, with anxieties, longings, needs. She is still in high school, full of inexperience, doesn't belong in a bordello.

I am appalled. It is wildly inappropriate that she be there. She has made a terrible mistake, has fallen into evil hands, is in trouble. How could those men, the ones who rumpled the sheets, how could they have done to her such things as I am forced by this setting to imagine? Had they no common decency? Could they not see she was a child? Did they not know this would destroy her? Did they not care?

Anger is rising in me. I am moving up to the bed, am standing beside it, taking Joan's hand. Now I turn, am facing the men who might still be wanting her, am denying her to them, making them ashamed of what they intended with her. Now I am telling her to get dressed, I am taking her out of here. No one will stop me. She will go back home with me, to her own room, will go back to school. When she finishes high school, she will go on to college, will prepare herself for a vocation, for a way of life that will sustain self-respect.

Now I position the paper to reflect the prostitute. She is quite young, but is awakened, not a virgin, has been through quite a few romps, is becoming wanton, yet still is in the first flowering, a bit bewildered by so much passion. That slight confusion and helplessness, that pliant vulnerability, excites me. No will of her own; I can do as I like. Her resistance, to anything, will be slight. I will override her objections, will ride her down. She will know she should stop me, yet will not. Something about me will make her want to give in, to do as I wish.

I feel the mounting excitement of a hunter closing in on his prey; I don't want to hurt her, but to have her, to ravish her. I will be gentle. I sit on the bed, begin to stroke her face, her cheeks rounded like a child's, her short curly hair. She is a bit frightened but likes my touch. I move on to her breasts, her belly, gradually escalate my violation of her unspoken limits, move always toward the center, breaching the concentric defenses one after another, coming in from the perimeter, moving always toward the center. I play with her nipples, make them stand up, suck them, explore the crevices of her belly button. Her will is paralyzed, she cannot resist. I continue my excursions into ever more forbidden recesses, proceeding inexorably, as a foregone certainty known to us both, to that eventual pulling apart of her legs and plunging into her cunt. She is an object, not a subject. I see not *her* need, but her capacity to serve *my* need. And what is my need? To do to her something like what a farmer does to the land. Take it over, seize possession, plow into it, seed it, make it grow. The farmer does not trouble himself with whether it is in the interest of the land to receive such treatment; nor do I with this pliant young woman.

What can I make of this? Do I have any answers? Am I doomed to be one or the other, protector or predator? Is there no other way with her? Where is love? Indeed, *what* is love? And where in this scenario might it have appeared? . . . I shift the paper, the fall of light alternating the images. Is love the fusion of these two orientations? A fusion that in my life has fallen apart? Or is it a third position unknown to me, beyond my reach?

WHEN I VIEW my daughter I enter a relationship, deal with a person. When I view the prostitute I abandon human relations, dismember her, deal with parts: breasts, buttocks, belly, genitals. She shatters like a pane of glass into erotic shards, into mounds and curves and apertures. What am I clawing after so desperately over these surfaces? For love? With a shard?

We strain toward an unattainable closeness. No way further to invade her, any her, no deeper plunge. We've had our way with her, have done everything, yet desire still clamors, is thrown back, baffled, by the gentle yielding flesh. One must give up. To go further is madness.

Madmen kill. It *must* be there, they think, somewhere within that supple body . . . the secret, the mystery. Why can it not be found or reached or touched? They won't stop. But murder has no longer reach than love, and madmen too are defeated, stand empty-handed, bereft, before the dismembered body, the still-warm heart.

We drape fantasies over women, making them into something they are not. They look up at us from magazines, the garment gapes, the flesh gleams; we see them from the rear, they glance back invitingly, shyly, alluringly, wearing rags and tags of black lace, bending over, pulling on a stocking.

They are pure receptivity. They are *our* fantasies, yet look real, as if they were out there somewhere, to be found, and we believe that with such a one that merging, that oneness, might be possible. Maybe *she*—that one in the purple garter belt—would welcome the pursuit, the capture, the being held close, being taken possession of, and all the rest of what we would want to do with her. And maybe *she* would, but she's not real.

And if, in a fit of mad enterprise, we should contact the agent of that model, and eventually after much embarrassment should manage to meet her . . . she's wearing jeans, is reticent, opinionated, stubborn, a bit suspicious, doesn't even own a garter belt.

And even if, as the wildest improbability, we should find a woman who had become the fantasy . . . even then the sought-for closeness would not be possible. For the woman who really matched the fantasy would be empty. Nothing there.

There's something really crazy about men. I mean about sex. They lose all sense of proportion. Can't see it simply as a good thing. They bring it up close, put it right in front of their noses . . . then they can't see anything else, it blots out the world. Women aren't like that. I'm not like that. If he's tired for a few nights, or preoccupied or worried, whatever, it's no matter to me. What's important is whether he's nice to me. If he notices me, if he talks to me, if he cares. Then it doesn't matter if we don't make love for a while. But with him, if I'm tired or preoccupied—just let that go on for a few nights—then, no matter how nice I am to him in every other way, it's no go. He gets cold, distant, gloomy. Lets me know in every possible way he's hurting. You'd think I'd betrayed him with his best friend. And nothing will help. Nothing but one thing. Throwing him a piece of ass. The sun comes out. The sky turns blue, meaning comes back into life.

You know what it is? He'd never admit it. May not know it. His desire is a sin. Not sex in general, not desire in other people. His. But he endows me with the authority to absolve him. If I, independently, want him to do to me what he already has in mind to do to me—if I crave it—he regains innocence. In my depravity! Then for a while he is at peace with himself, on good terms with God. That's why that gratitude after an orgasm. I have restored him to grace. And that's what makes his desire so driven and compulsive. If it were just glands and hormones, it'd be simple. Like in animals. Would come and go. Would be simply one part of life. It's not like that for him. The other way round. Glands and hormones have been drafted by his scheme for salvation. They work overtime. Day and night. It's not carnal at all but metaphysical. Salvation for a sinner like him is a never-ending task.

COLLETTE: "LISTENING IS an effort that ages the face, makes the neck muscles ache, and stiffens the eyelids looking fixedly at the speaker. It is a kind of studied debauch . . . Not only the listening, but the interpreting . . . the elevating to its secret meaning a litany of dull words, promoting acrimony to grief or wild desire."

SOMETIMES IT SEEMS that all my analyzing, which aims to control experience, is but a shadow play on the surface of experience. It controls nothing, it but measures my demand that experience be understandable. Life trips me; I am in a maze, every day a new mystery. I wrap interpretations around the peculiar shapes that impact on me, try to subjugate them, reduce them to order. I *clothe* experience. Presented with a hunchback, I can, good tailor that I am, cut a coat to fit; but my coats correct no deformities, nor tell me anything of the peculiar shape of the next customer I shall have to deal with.

> *Violation is part of my desire, the dark underside. Might be better not to know. But I do know. The garden must be secret, guarded, mysterious. Access must be hidden or difficult or denied. I seek to enter where, though I be desired, I'm not altogether welcome. Resistance must be overcome. Some advantage, not entirely fair or honorable, must be taken.*
>
> *The veiled face, that's the archetype. It signals both resistance and invitation, the one as important as the other. Of course that veil has been displaced upward. It's really the genital that is veiled, and the veil is to be rent. Not the open, smiling face. Not the pretty cheerleader at a football game with bare legs, prancing about, grinning; but the elegant lady in velvet and fur glimpsed for but a moment as she gets out of a cab. Or, better, from a carriage. Carriage? Why is that better? Because in the days of carriages, gardens were better guarded, their despoliation more difficult, hence a keener pleasure. The driver stops the horses before a handsome three-story house with shuttered windows, an air of mystery; the door of the carriage opens, a little boy gets out, a muffled cry from within, the boy turns back, a woman leans out, lifts her veil—the veil! that's central—she clasps the boy to her breast, kisses him wildly, her face covered with tears. Why tears? What does that add? I've come upon her in a moment of weakness; and that weakness nourishes my wish to violate, adds a pulse of hope.*
>
> *┼I can't believe it's this way for women. They don't want to violate a man. Were one of them to approach me with the motivation I bring to them, I'd run for my life. Or for my soul! What*

This statement moves me from fantasy to the fact … the eyes of the woman before me.

they want must be something quite different. They want to be talked to. I know what they want. They want to be understood, to be known in their specialness, to be truly recognized.

THIS VIOLATION GETS filtered out in marriage. It becomes shameful, is excluded. It's a lie that the full range of physical love can be realized in marriage. Conjugal love has comforts and advantages, and convenience, but this transcendent passion, dependent on a trace of predation, it has not. When a man has free access, the garden no longer secret, there is no remaining mystery. When it stands open, is repeatedly known, when he enters at will, traverses the same old paths, comes time and again upon the same old vistas, then he is in the realm of daily bread, of affection and security, of a "good relationship." And all that may be very good indeed, may be the best we can hope for, and it may be that a wise man would settle for such. All that may be true. But it's not true that it's the same as that first knowing, that primal surrender and that primal violation. Not only does this not occur in marriage, it's not possible in principle. It's a lie. It's the publicity line for the guardians of our sacred institutions, who would have us believe that a faithful marriage does not entail the giving up of something magical and mysterious in the life of the flesh.

A FEARLESS WOMAN is without attraction. Admirable perhaps, worthy, resourceful, a loyal friend, all those good things; but for that magic that pulls us on, sucks our hearts out, she must be vulnerable.

I will never forget the Spanish girl. Blue uniform, like an airline hostess. Small blue pillbox cap on her head, straight brown hair to the level of her chin, one strand falling across her right eye as she lowers her head. Enormous dark liquid eyes. Great shyness. Afraid to look, to make eye contact, yet willing if it is required, then quickly the frightened smile, the averted gaze.

"Life is vulgar. Pursuit of the vulgar is loyalty to life." She puts on her martyr face. "This is gutter talk. You're not like that. You have always been one to search for the spiritual." "I was brainwashed. The gutter is all there is."

AT MY GRANDFATHER'S house in Marion, the outhouse was rickety, damp, rank with urine, shit, and lime. A bushel basket of crinkled squares of tissue paper, the paper oranges used to be wrapped in. Kleber brought them home from the store. I remember once, having shat, standing up and looking down the hole, seeing a faint glimmer of liquid surface. Then, as the sun aligned itself with a crack in the footing, a shaft of light revealed that surface to be, not still as I had supposed, but alive, writhing with maggots. In the stillness I could hear the faint licking sound of their movements in the muck.

I stared with the fascination of one who sees the future. We rise up out of the earth and assume the shape of God. Briefly, briefly. Then down into the earth again. The handful of me I had just dropped in that pit was already being transformed into maggots, and presently they would get the rest of me. I would become them. Their writhing would be my writhing.

In the meantime, then, in that crack of light, as Nabokov puts it, between two eternities of darkness, maybe the best we can do is our own special writhing together, which alone has the power to blot out for a moment the darkness and the worms.

THE FLYING DUTCHMAN

THERE IS A fecal smell in this room. On the bed, unconscious, my mother is slowly bleeding to death from the bowel.
Over the radio, faintly, Mahler's Fourth Symphony. I have
switched off the light. Outside the window the shadowy gestures of poplars.

Daylight says life is knowable, night tells the truth, says we
know not what lies hidden, neither in the darkness out there
nor the darkness within. Day is pragmatic acceptance, night is
infinite longing.

All of life is here: the smell of shit, the sound of music, the
surrounding dark.

WE LOOK INTO the deaths of others, even much-loved others,
as in a dark mirror. We seek a glimpse of our own.

MY MOTHER IS one hundred years old, has been dying for a long time. For years. Two months ago, I was called by the nursing home; that was perhaps the beginning of the end.

She has stopped eating, the nurse tells me. She sits at the table in her wheelchair, pushes the food about with her spoon. If the nurses put it in her mouth, she spits it out. If they persist, she becomes cross. Occasionally she will swallow a few bites of ice cream.

I speak to her on the telephone: "I am coming to see you soon, Mother. I *want* you to eat. Are you listening? Mother? You *must* eat—so you will be strong for my visit." A few days later a call from her doctor: she has lost a lot of weight, he wants to hospitalize her, to begin force-feeding. I refuse. She is confused, I tell him, could not possibly understand what was being done to her, would be terrified by the tube in her throat. I speak again to the nurses: "Offer her small amounts. Frequently. Encourage her to eat. But don't force her."

I try to speak to her on the phone, hear the nurse say, "Hold it to your ear, Mrs. Wheelis. It's your son!" "Mother!" I yell into the phone. "Mother! Can you hear me?" She drops the phone in her lap, mumbles unintelligibly.

When I arrive, she is not in her room. I glance in the open door. Her blue mohair shawl lies in a heap on the bed. I go looking for her—in the halls, in the TV room—return presently to discover that my mother herself lies beneath the crumpled shawl. A tangle of bones in a bag of skin. Her body makes no impression on the bed.

I take her hand, call her name, shake her slightly. The smeared eyes open blankly. "Mother, it's me. Your son. It's Allen." Suddenly the skeleton hand tightens on mine, a smile comes to her face. She struggles to lift herself, to turn toward me. She falls back, but presently, out of that waste, two stick arms rise up to embrace me.

I stay with her three days. From my hand, when I command

it, she will eat. Constantly I am lifting something to her mouth, urging on her yet another sip of liquid protein. She gains some strength, is able to talk, can sit up for a few minutes.

WHY, AS I hold this vigil, do I keep thinking of the island in Puget Sound? Is that where I will die?

I remember a gleaming night last fall. I am lying in bed in darkness. I stretch, sink into luxurious softness, relax. Ilse is asleep beside me. The cedar branch waves sleepily before the window; the Sound is a ghostly silver under a cloudy sky. A sighing wind in the tall trees, the whisper of surf. I am suffused with a deep pleasure, happiness, a sense of power, of control. The long day just finished passes in review. Discontinuously. *Click, click, click*—like snapshots. Twenty hours earlier, at the beginning of this long day, I was lying in darkness, in just such a bed, not relaxed but poised for flight. That was in Hotel Margna, Sils Baselgia, in the Upper Engadin of Switzerland. It is just before five in the morning. I have, as always before a long journey, waked before the alarm clock sounds. *Click, click, click.* Going up the serpentine Julier Pass I catch a glimpse of a trailer truck coming down, two turns away, but coming too fast. I pull off the road and wait. As it roars by, brakes squealing, it occupies the entire road. *Click, click, click.* I am at the Air France counter in Zurich, waiting to check in. The line doesn't move. I sense a strange restlessness and inactivity in the staff; they are waiting for something. "There's going to be a strike," I whisper to my wife. "This plane won't leave." We move quickly, get the last two seats on a Swissair flight to Boston. *Click, click, click.* The camera focuses now on a moment six hours ago: On a winding road near Tacoma, an oil rig overtakes me spilling oil. I stop. Other cars pass by me. "Why are we stopping?" my wife asks. Presently, up ahead, the cars spin out of control on the widening slick. I turn back, take a detour. *Click, click, click.* The camera is trained on the present moment. I am euphoric because of my quickness, my control of contingency. I glance at my sleeping wife. I have lofted her as on a perfectly aimed ballistic missile, halfway around the world, and there she is safe, asleep.

The Sound is a gleaming silver, the moon winks, and presently something other drifts in on the sighing wind. *Click, click, click,* this camera won't stop. I control nothing, am being swept away; a few more clicks and you'll search the frames for me in vain.

WHAT WE DENY is not death but the awareness that, before we die, nothing is going to happen. That big vague thing, that redemptive fulfillment, is an illusion, a beckoning bribe to keep us loyal. A symphony has a climax, a poem builds to a burst of meaning, but we are unfinished business. No coming together of strands. The game is called because of darkness.

WHEN I DIE I want my body to be cremated, the ashes buried in the orchard on the island in Puget Sound, the site marked by a flat stone of green marble bearing my name and dates, and a small distance below, my paradox.

> How to live?
> Who knows the question knows not how,
> Who knows not the question cannot tell.

Those three lines sum me up: the inquiry that has driven me, and the impasse into which it has invariably delivered me.

I choose the orchard because there, among those gnarled and broken apple trees, blossoming unseen on the empty air, dropping their wormy and unwanted fruit for the deer and the crows, the loamy land sloping down to the slough, the blue heron standing motionless on one long spindly leg, mirrored in the still water, the steely blue Sound beyond, and far away on the horizon the jagged Olympic Mountains icy, snow-covered, distant—there, at times, I've had a sense of home.

Actually I would prefer to be buried there, my body intact, in a plain cedar box. But that's hard to arrange; and, as between lying intact among strangers in a cemetery or lying in ashes and bone fragments in that magical place, I choose the latter.

And I can see it coming about. Soon. I shall not have long to wait. And when it is done, my wishes all exactly met by a loving and respectful family, it will gratify me not at all; for the consciousness that now wills it and is capable of gratification by it will have vanished. Indeed, it would matter naught to me, at that time, were my body thrown into the garbage. I am carefully arranging something that cannot possibly become a reality until its fulfillment shall have become unknowable to me. So any brooding on that site, any ghostly gratification, must be claimed in advance. Now.

So . . . this is the future scene to which I suppose I am now laying claim. A late summer afternoon, the sun disappearing behind the Olympics, the sawtooth ridge knifelike against a pale green sky, clouds red and gold, becoming pink turning to gray turning to black. Far far overhead, silently, a plane passes, leaving a glittering silver trail. A sloop with a blue sail glides past the beach. The heron rises ponderously from the slough, the great wings beating slowly, heavily, uttering his hoarse and protesting cry. From the table at the edge of the cliff near the house come voices, the sounds of dinner—my children and grandchildren, friends, dogs. Joan wanders alone down through the twilit orchard, glances at the green stone, reads again the pithy anguish of my life. I always wanted to write in stone: now I will have done so. She directs toward me a current of melancholy affection, reexperiences the quite special bond between us. The stone is partly covered by the long dry grass of autumn. I must clear that away, she thinks, plant some flowers. Perhaps tomorrow. She glances . . . and passes on . . . and that's all.

So—I can imagine all this. And my mother cannot. Does that make any difference?

Night falls.

That's all.

THESE ARE THE last hours of my mother's life. And she knows nothing. Only I observe her blind, stumbling arrival at the end of a century-long journey. I hope it may be different as I lie dying. I hope that I will be able to take myself as the object of reflection, see my life in extension, the whole course—taking off like a ballistic missile, soaring, leveling off, falling—and, just before the end, achieve, like the computer in a warhead at impact, a view of the whole trajectory.

I doubt my mother has ever done this, or would want to. For years now, she has had no awareness of death. Death got lost as memory failed and reality slipped away. The last time she grappled with it was six years ago. She was ninety-four, frail and failing. She took my hand, solemnly, between both of her own, her voice dropped, her manner became portentous. "Son, I want you to know . . . *you* know . . . I don't want to live forever . . . you know that . . . son, some folks nowadays . . . they just hang on and on, no use to themselves or anybody else, taking up space and costing money. I don't want anything like that. I don't want you to take any special measures . . . you know what I mean?"

"Yes, Mama, I know."

"I've lived a long time, and when my time comes . . . when it's right for me to go . . . well, I'm ready. I leave that all to you. It's up to you."

"I understand."

"I don't want to just hang on when my mind is gone and I'm no use to people."

"You're still in good health, Mama. You have a lot of life before you. I want you to keep living as long as you can enjoy things."

We sit in silence. She strokes my hand absently, brooding, troubled. Her breathing becomes irregular, she wants to speak. Can't find the right words. She sighs. "Son," she says after a bit, "son, tell me . . . how long do you think I will live?"

I realize she is afraid. "You have a lot of vitality, Mother. You've always been very strong . . . "

"That's true."

"You've pulled through bad sicknesses that would've been too much for most people."

"That's true."

"So I think you might . . . live to"—I canvass her anxious face, extend my estimate—"you'll probably live to be one hundred!" Wildly extravagant. But maybe she will buy it. Perhaps it will make her happy.

Her expression doesn't change. She fixes her eyes on mine, judiciously weighs, examines, my estimate: "That's not very long, you know."

IN ATTENDING MY mother's death I preview my own, try to get the feel of it, take its measure. But cannot, can never get this matter settled. I accept what's coming only in the sense of acknowledging its inevitability, not in affirming its propriety or rightness.

An uneasy truce, the terms are not clear. Something more should be possible. One should not be stuck forever with this nagging problem as unfinished business. How is it handled by the wise, by the really mature?

An interview on television with Erik Erikson. "And have you achieved wisdom, Mr. Erikson?" The question is loaded, for Erik has staked his reputation on the depiction of life as phasic; and the task of the last phase, in which his shaky infirmity unmistakably places him, presents the alternatives of wisdom and despair. "Have you achieved wisdom, Mr. Erikson?" He hesitates, then stands behind his product: "I'm afraid I have."

Mazeltov. I have not. I'm as old as he, almost. Anyway, like him slogging along through the last phase, if it *is* a phase, anyway the last years of life. But not with wisdom. Rather, with the vanity, awkwardness, longing, and sham that have characterized my passage through all the other phases.

I distrust the wisdom of old men. I listen to them and am not convinced. I suspect a coverup. They don't have things really straight either. They're headed, mapless, into the same dark that awaits us all.

We know what it is, we see it lying in wait up ahead: Consciousness is going to end. That vast net which, nearing the end of a long life, has acquired such enormous reach into time and space, such variety of experience, inward and outward, backward and forward, that knows so much, and, beyond what it knows, can imagine anything—consciousness, that ringing glass, is going to shatter, its shards plunge back into nothingness. Like the fading fragments of a burst of fireworks.

THE LIGHT SNAPS on. The nurse enters, opens the diaper. No feces now, just bright red blood. The nurse stares at me with a mute question: She wants to call an ambulance, wants my mother rushed to the hospital, to have a blood transfusion. I shake my head. She points to the hands and feet, which are turning blue. Again I shake my head. Her expression closes over with disapproval. She cleans my mother's wasted bottom, puts on a fresh diaper. Together, one on each side of the bed, we feel the pulse. It is weak and fast and thready. The nurse leaves.

SLOWLY MY EYES adapt to darkness. I see the faint line of gray molding around the ceiling. All is quiet. No bark of dog, no hum of traffic. Faint light of moon. It seems I have been running: I long to rest. I think of the island. It seems far away, long ago. Months ago. Yet in fact only days. A week ago we were there; we cleaned the house thoroughly as we always do, put everything away, locked up, left. It exists there now without us. Eight hundred miles away. Deserted, still, silent. Remote, dreamlike.

I call it back, I drift toward it, and presently it seems I am actually there. Moonlight on the moss-covered shakes; the white siding gleams brightly. I stand at the edge of the cliff. The Sound is still, a faint lapping at the shore below. The moon beats a straight wake from Mount Rainier across the water to me.

Now I enter the house. I am a ghost, enter without unlocking or opening doors. Moonlight gleams on the polished oak floor. I pause to marvel at the vast depth of the silence. A scurrying sound in the chimney, and a chipmunk appears. Apparently I am neither seen nor felt, for the chipmunk moves calmly over, or perhaps through, my foot. The rug is rolled up and put away, all the cushions are in plastic bags, the wall hangings are in the closet, the thermostat is set at sixty degrees just as I left it. Everything cool, still. I pass through the closed door, walk down the path to the beach, sit in the sand, watch the moon rise in the sky, grow whiter, smaller.

The sky lightens. I walk back up the path. Now everything is different. Bright sunshine. People moving about. I see through the windows the wall hangings in place. An outdoor table has been set up; people are eating. Ah, I know this scene. This is Joan's birthday party two weeks ago. There I am, sitting at the head of the table, facing, as always, down toward the orchard and the rugged Olympic Mountains to the north. All of my family is here. Ilse; Joan and her husband, Pablo; Mark and his wife, Katy, and their children, Emily and Ian; Vicki and her sons, Austin and Noah. And our old friends Phyllis and

Otto. I watch myself sitting there, carving, pouring wine, eating, am amused to see myself thus, also somewhat uncomfortable, did not realize I was so stooped, so old and frail, in speech so modest, so uncertain.

My self at the table is unaware of my presence as a ghost. I walk about unseen, unheard, hear myself at the table saying those things I remember saying two weeks ago. And presently Emily, on request, sings her little song, "I'd rather have a Buick, a Buick," just as she did then.

I leave the festive scene, wander about the orchard. How I love this place! I walk up the sloping path to the mailboxes. An old woman is approaching, coming down the gravel road. Haggard face, stringy gray hair, slender, somewhat bent over but still quite tall. She limps slightly, but seems anyway to be hurrying, something of eagerness about her, of tense anticipation.

Suddenly I realize that this is Mrs. Stringer. So she is a ghost, too. Died about 1950. My house now was her house then. She left it to her son, Herbert Spahr. He sold it to me in 1962. All through the lonely Depression years, all through the heavy war years, Mrs. Stringer lived here alone. Phyllis would occasionally stop by. Mrs. Stringer had the only phone on the island, and she loved to have people come to use it. These were the only times she had anyone to talk to. The visitor would have to socialize a bit before using the phone. Mrs. Stringer would eavesdrop on the call itself, and then there would be a little chat at the end. She was a great gossip.

She passes by me now and starts down the sloping path. Her pace slows. What once was an open sunny way is now a tunnel through arching trees. I see her shock as she notices that the barn is gone. There is nothing there. And a further shock on glancing to the right and seeing an enormous new barn where once was the old well. She walks on more slowly, shaken. The house at least will be as she remembers. It's not changed. But no, she looks in through the open front door, gives a start, decides not to enter, goes on around the corner of the house to where Joan's birthday party is in progress.

She stops suddenly, stands there searching the company. As her eyes rest on Phyllis, I see a glimmer of recognition, which then fades. All are strange. She is looking for her son. Dismay deepens on her face. I see her lips form his name. No one hears. She knows no one. There is no place for her here. She turns to leave. At the corner of the house she pauses, looks back, moves on. I follow her. She is plodding up the path toward the mailboxes, stooped, tired, bereft. I feel for her, want to mitigate this usurpation. It *was* her home. I call, but she cannot hear. I take her arm, but she is as immaterial as I. No body, no contact, no comfort. She disappears in the dark of trees.

I am deeply troubled. She seemed to know that much time had passed, that things would be different. Yet still she hoped to find a place here. Her son would surely be here, and his children, whom she knew when they were little, and now also, perhaps, her great-grandchildren, whom she would not know but who would look familiar. She would have a place. And that glance into the living room, that sudden not-entering. The wallpaper—of course! Gone. She had picked it out herself, a great find. Dark green with pink flamingos, her great pride. She had pointed it out to everyone who stopped by to use the phone. I recall our own disdain. The first thing we did on acquiring this place was to rip it off, all of us, the whole family, stripping it away, vandalizing the room with a kind of scornful hilarity. We then paneled the walls with burlap and Philippine mahogany. That's why she didn't enter. It no longer looked like her house. And her son was not here. Only strangers.

As I come back around the corner of the house, I sense a change. Yet there is the company of people around the table, the family party. But somehow everything is different. Suddenly I see that I am no longer sitting there at the head of the table. Someone else is in my place. And this is not my family! These are strangers. Adults and children. What are they doing here? An old woman in a wheelchair is off to one side. The others seem to ignore her. Something else is different. The tree at the edge of the cliff, the big Douglas fir. Where is it? It has disappeared as if by magic. Not a trace. The edge of the cliff itself has moved, is now six feet closer to the house. It would take fifty years for that much erosion. I walk down in the orchard. The trees are gone. I look for the green stone. The place is overgrown with blackberry creepers. The stone is not to be found. I float back to the party. They have rolled the old lady onto the porch. Her withered hands flutter about the wheels; she wants to be with them in the party, within the sound of human voices. Her eyes are milky with cataracts. My God! My daughter, Joan! My lissome child! I cry out, fall to the ground at her knees. She cannot hear me, cannot see me, I cannot reach her.

THE LAST TIME I came to visit, a few weeks ago, my mother was hallucinating.

"Oh! Oh! Look at that rain . . . how it's coming down. Close the window, son. Quick! Before everything is under water."

"It's all right, Mother. It's not raining. Nothing will get wet."

"The levee may not hold. See about the horses, son! Mama! Mama!" She lifts herself slightly. "Where's my mama, son?"

"She died a long time ago."

She falls back, sighs. "Ah yes. Ah yes. I remember now . . . Araminta Matilda Black. Do you remember her? Poisoned her husband. Said she didn't mean to, though. She was born in the spring during the high water and was buried on the banks of the Ouachita near Careyville. Smoke! Where is all that smoke coming from? Must be a terrible fire. I can't make out a thing. Gather up the valuables, son! Call the marshal!"

A DAY LATER.

"There's something wrong down here, son." She pushes at the bedclothes.

"Do you have pain?"

"No. A kind of itch, a burning."

"I'll ask the nurse to get you something."

"They don't know about such things. I've already told them. They don't know."

"Well, I'll ask your doctor."

"You're my doctor, son. Remember? You saved my life. Twice. If it weren't for you, I wouldn't be here today." She has pushed down the covers, is pulling up her nightgown. "Have a look, son. See what you think."

"No, Mother, it's better that . . ."

"It's all right for you to look, son. You're a doctor."

She opens her legs, raises her knees. Her belly has disappeared, is draped against her spine; the aorta throbs visibly beneath the blotchy yellowish skin. Mons veneris has disappeared: no more that spongy rounded mound, no more that thicket of dark hair. A few spare tufts of white sprout from the bare bone of pubis. No flesh anywhere to be seen. The buttocks have vanished; the skin which once covered those ample cheeks now falls from the iliac crests as a gray curtain, pools on the sheet like candlewax. The bony architecture of the pelvis looms up from the mattress like a ruined and haunted house—of which I am the appalled ghost.

"SON . . . COME CLOSER. There's something we must talk about." I sit on the edge of the bed. She takes my hand, holds it between both her own, strokes it, looks away into the distance. She is thinking, wants me to be prepared for a weighty matter. The bones of her hands are covered with a yellowish film with dark brown blotches. No flesh remains; the papery skin with its tangle of black veins sinks in between the bones.

"Son"—she focuses on me, lowers her voice—"son, we've been associated together a long time. And so it's only natural . . . that we have become very *fond* of each other. It's been a very long . . . and a very close . . . association. And so, after all that time . . . it's only natural . . . we might want to get married. . . . " She pauses. "We don't have to do it right away, though. No need to rush into anything. But it's only natural."

"I'm already married, Mother."

"You're already married?"

"Yes."

"Who is your wife? What is her *name*, son?"

"Ilse. Do you remember Ilse?"

"Well, would she be . . . jealous?"

"Yes."

"Well, we certainly don't want to upset her. We don't want that. We just won't rush into anything."

"Mother, listen! We can't get married. You're my *mother*, I'm your *son!*"

"Yes, well . . . that's true, that's certainly true, and we've been very close, very close together . . . for a very long time. That's true, isn't it?"

"Yes."

"But we don't want to upset anyone. We mustn't cause a stir. But I want to tell you something, son." She strokes my hand tenderly. "We have plenty of time. No need to rush into anything. So, if you want to look around first, try out some of the younger girls . . . see how you like it . . . if you want to do that . . . I want you to know, I won't mind. You look around all you like. I'll wait for you."

HER BREATHING NOW is a labored rattle. The legs are blue to above the knees, the arms to above the elbows. I cannot feel a pulse.

THE ASTONISHED BIRD flies upward, high, high, away from its strangely burning feet. Alights on a telephone wire, falls forward, with spread wings catches itself, flies to the branch of a tree, falls forward, tries again, falls, and again, again. Now it flutters motionless in air, hovers like an osprey above a branch, lowers itself vertically, with a beating of wings, touches down, falls backward, flutters to another branch, falls forward. Presently it alights on a shelf of leaves, finds itself resting, but not on its feet; the legs without feet have dropped between the twigs. The wings beat helplessly against the leaves. Presently it falls clear, again is airborne, alights on a branch, falls forward, to another, falls, falls, falls. Trees and earth have become hostile. Now it soars up, up, as if to leave them behind, to find another realm, high in the darkening sky. But is getting weak, cannot sustain itself, is drifting down again to resume its agony. The swoops from branch to branch become shorter, lower. Presently it drops to the top of a bush, finds itself enmeshed in branches. It cannot move. Children play nearby, mothers call; it is time to go home. The bird flutters, drops deeper in the bush, is trapped. A dog hears the flutter, is sniffing; a black nose pushes its way into the bush. The wings flutter violently; the bird drops lower and lower. The dog sniffs. Presently the bird fights clear of the lowest branches, falls to the ground. The nose is upon it, the whiskers quiver, the nostrils dilate. The dog's eyes, intent with curiosity, are without malice, without pity, without mercy. The mouth opens on large teeth. The frantic bird flutters, rolls; the dog follows. Presently the wings gain the air, carry the bird again aloft and away from the open mouth. It flies up to a branch, falls, catches itself, to another, falls, and if one could follow the path of this desperate bird through the darkening afternoon one would find hundreds of branches marked with two tiny red dots.

It is weak now, cannot fly up, alights on the bar of a children's turnabout, falls, hits the platform with a thud, rolls to the sand. It flutters this way and that, zigzag, out of the sand, gains the air, but cannot rise. It flies a foot or so above the ground, alights on a concrete walk, falls forward, beak hitting the stone. Again and again it flies and alights, again and again the beak striking the stone. The eyes are glazed; a trickle of blood runs from the beak. The flutter of wings subsides, is finally still. It is night. A rising wind stirs the feathers.

I DRIVE SLOWLY through the cemetery. Winter. A cold clear day, blue sky, weak noonday sun. The trees are barren, the grass dry and withered. The gray stones gleam dully, strewn as if at random in the sloping brown meadow. In the distance a hearse, a black-suited man waiting nearby. He notices my hesitation, starts toward me. I stop the car. We get out, I introduce my family, he leads the way.

We come to a blue awning mounted on poles, open on all sides, covering the grave. I recognize the coffin I selected at the funeral home. It rests on green canvas slings within a chrome frame. Beneath the frame, a green carpet simulating grass. We approach. "Not too close," the director cautions. I sense the black void beneath the fake grass. We stand in silence before the casket. Beside my feet is a flat gray stone.

DR. M. B. WHEELIS
1882–1925

The director whispers to me: "Shall I?" I nod. He opens the upper segment of the casket lid.

On a billowy white bed lies my mother, exposed to us now from the waist up. She wears a striped silk blouse that my wife bought for her years ago. Her head is elevated on a white ruffled pillow, her white hair nicely combed, her face powdered and rouged. Her mouth and eyes are closed. The lines of care and of anxiety have been wiped smooth.

We stare at her. "She looks more serene in death," I say, "than ever in life." We shift about slightly, uneasily, but remain facing her. The funeral director appears again; he wants to know if others will be coming, perhaps a minister. "No one else," I say, then add, "We will stand here a while . . . and talk." He nods, retreats. After a while I begin to speak.

"I want to say something . . . in tribute to my mother . . . lest those qualities of hers deserving of tribute be lost. And they *might* be lost, for they were not much in evidence in recent years. In 1947, she had a long and serious illness . . . almost died, never fully recovered. She was fifty-eight. That's when she began to be old. And she became—finally—a foolish and pathetic old woman. Foolish in her doting . . . and erotized adoration of me, and in her constant exaggeration of my virtues and my accomplishments . . . And mean-spirited in her invidious denigration of my sister."

I am speaking softly, with long unintended pauses, as if wanting someone to break in. The four others incline their heads slightly toward me.

"But once the colors of her life were more vivid. And that's what I want to recall . . . and to evoke."

That's not true, I think; the colors of her life were always gray.

"Her father was a man of immense authority . . . in his community and in . . . his family. And no one was more respectful of that authority than my mother. But when she fell in love, she found the strength to oppose him. 'I forbid you to marry this man,' her father said. 'He will never have anything, and he will die young of tuberculosis.' As it turned out, he was right— on both counts. But my mother followed her heart. Because of her father's opposition, she could not be married at home or even in the same town. But one day my father pulled up in a buggy, and my mother walked out of her father's house and they drove off to Farmersville and were married by the justice of the peace. So . . . one must say of her . . . she was a woman capable of independent action."

That, too, is a lie. Why am I standing here with my family telling lies? Never on her own did she defy her father. When *my* father came along and she fell in love, she simply transferred her dependence to him; and on *his* authority, in obedience to *his* will, walked out of her father's house.

"And in 1937 in Marion a black man named Norris was beaten by Joe Turner, the farmer who employed him. Norris had left the gate open, and the cows had got into the garden . . . and Joe Turner was a man with a bad temper. At that time, in that place, a black man did not fight back, for that would invite a lynching. He just took it—stoically or perhaps begging for mercy. So Norris stood and took his beating: broken jaw, missing teeth, broken shoulder. The town regarded such an incident with tolerance—amused tolerance by some ("That'll teach ole Norris a lesson! Guess it'll be a spell 'fore he leaves that gate open again!"), disapproving tolerance by others. The sheriff certainly wasn't going to do anything about it.

My mother tried to get my uncle Kleber to act, but he didn't want to tangle with Joe Turner. So nothing was done. But one day . . . on a Saturday about noon . . . in the middle of the town square . . . with people milling about . . . my mother accosted Joe Turner. 'I know what you did,' she said, 'and it was an evil thing, a mean and cruel thing. This town, it looks like, will do nothing about it, but I hope God will punish you.' And so . . . she was a woman capable of acting alone . . . on principle."

I wasn't there. That's the story. Mit told me. Perhaps there's something to it. I made up the words, but perhaps she did say something, maybe not at noon, not in the town square, maybe not even to Joe Turner directly, but *something*. Every life holds some myth of heroism, and I credit hers with this brave confrontation.

"When my father developed tuberculosis he was advised to

go west, and they moved here, to San Antonio. He could have remained indefinitely in a veterans hospital, but my mother knew that he would have a better chance at home. So they bought a house and she brought him home and nursed him. For six years she cooked for him, brought his meals, bathed him, dressed him, burned the sputum cups, carried the bedpans, and boiled the sheets of his bed in an iron pot over a wood fire in the backyard. And all this, while taking care also of her children—in good spirit and without complaint. And so . . . one must say of her, she was a woman capable of unusual loyalty . . . and devotion . . . and self-sacrifice."

All this is true. Finally, something I'm saying is true.

"And when, one October morning, just after daybreak . . . yellow sunlight streaming in horizontally through the windows, glinting on my father's upturned and now waxen face . . . everyone waiting speechless, breathless . . . the doctor straightened up, folded his stethoscope, and said, 'He's gone,' there burst forth from my mother's throat a scream, so loud . . . so terrifying . . . the sound of a large animal that has been struck a mortal blow . . . a scream that tore through me like a spear . . . and she reeled back, flailing wildly, falling . . . and a few days later at this very spot . . . her anguished sobs as his body was lowered. And so . . . one must say of her . . . she was a woman capable of passion and of pain."

Of pain certainly. Of pain there was a lot. Of passion, I'm not so sure. Passion and desire she ascribed to men, making of herself an object, the obedient and responsive object of the will of her father, her husband, and her son. Of these three I had her the longest, am therefore most responsible for the shape of her life.

I end in a whisper, look about at my family. They are huddled around me, heads inclined toward me. They have been hanging in my net of words. Now that I have stopped, they are falling anxiously inward.

Is this woman a / woman / been / objects / to him / as well? [handwritten marginal note]

I signal to the funeral director that we are ready. He starts to close the casket. My wife takes my arm: "I want to say something." She fumbles, finds the pocket, extracts a piece of paper. I motion to the director to wait. "As I was thinking—" She bursts into tears. Presently, after a pause, she makes a new start. "As I was thinking what words to speak today, four lines from a Chinese poem came to mind:

> Man lives but once
> and never he returns.
> Life is like a breath of air
> that wafts away.

"But only our bodies don't return—so there will be room for others to live and to remember." Tears are streaming down her face. "Therefore I want to mourn Grandma's death by celebrating the lives of those who will contain her memory—her much-loved son, my husband, and our wonderful children, her grandchildren. May you live long and remember her fondly."

Mark, weeping, says a few words. Vicki, dry-eyed, speaks briefly. We stand in silence. I glance at Joan. She looks strained, choked; her eyes are large and shining. She shakes her head. Again I signal to the director that we are ready. Again he starts to close the casket. Joan whispers to me something I don't understand. "What?" She takes my arm, brings her mouth to my ear: "Her head is too high." Still I don't understand. She points to the white satin above my mother's face: "It's hitting her *nose!*"

I see then a smudge of makeup on the white lining of the casket lid. My daughter Joan! In matters of this kind the unchallenged Mistress of Protocol. When her goldfish died, she positioned the tiny glittering body in water, in seaweed, in the exact horizontal, as if still alive and swimming; and her hamster in death was arranged in his box in the exact posture in which, in life, it had slept. We are delivering the body of her grandmother to the worms, but so long as it is in our care, she will not permit that nose to be crowded.

At my request the funeral director rearranges the pillow, lowers my mother's head, then closes the casket.

We are asked to move back. Workmen appear, lift the chrome frame, slide out the green carpet. The grave yawns below—clean-cut walls of black earth, cut roots. Six feet down is an open concrete box, approximating the walls of the grave. The workmen bend to the winches. The chrome rollers turn, the green canvas sling unrolls, the coffin descends jerkily. A workman with a slender pole guides the casket into the box. With a muted thud it comes to rest. The slings are freed and withdrawn, the chrome frame removed. We stand at the edge, staring down.

"I'm afraid this will be noisy," the funeral director says, and moves us back. A gas engine starts up with a rattling clatter, and a small tractor comes chugging toward us pushing a wheeled frame within which is suspended a flat concrete slab. The frame is maneuvered over the grave. The winch turns; the lid is lowered, guided into position. The body within the coffin, within the concrete box, is now twice removed from us, is being sealed further and further away.

Again we are asked to move back. The tent is struck, poles and lines are stashed, the canvas folded, loaded into a cart. Pale winter sunlight falls around us, the pale winter sky spreads out above. Again the startup of a motor, again the chugging tractor, this time pulling a dumpster of black soil. It maneuvers with difficulty between the stones, backs the dumpster to the edge of the grave. Here now, without deceptive green, is the hidden piano of sixty-five years ago. The player has vanished, the melody is lost.

I am given a shovel. I reach up over the edge of the cart, take a shovelful of dirt. After a moment of hesitation, staring down, I deliver the soil. It swishes softly on the concrete slab. I take some slight comfort that the coffin itself is shielded from this falling earth. My wife follows, then each of my tall children, each in turn with a shovelful of earth.

XII

RACKETY-RACKETY-RACKETY

In bed, alone, in darkness, waiting for sleep, falling away in
the rustle of time, I dream: *I am a prisoner in a concentration
camp. My back has been broken. A guard offers me a pillow. I
decline. Presently he offers again. Moved by his kindness, I accept,
and immediately feel a blessed relief. All of the prisoners sit or lie
along the ramparts of the castle, all of us in an extremity of exhaustion from torture. I look down a sheer stone wall, several hundred
feet. A man is looking up at us, calling, chanting, waving his arms.
He wears a white shirt, blue jeans, sneakers. And a black cap. Has
long hair. A young man. Several guards in brown shirts stand
about watching him, occasionally looking up at us. The man sways
and beckons, utters long singing calls: "Come to me! Jump! It's so
easy. So-o-o easy. You will float through the air. Like a leaf. Like a
feather. No more pain. Never again will you suffer."*

I feel my own pain, also the wonderful softness of the pillow still at my back. I think of jumping, am tempted. I want to jump. Presently one of the prisoners does jump, plummets to his death on the rocks below. The one who beckons, encouraged now, renews and intensifies his call. His seductiveness becomes more insistent, ecstatic. Others jump. One by one they are crushed, like eggs, on the rocks. I want to follow, but hesitate—feel the softness at my back.

Then, in quick succession, still dreaming, I have three insights. First: In giving me the pillow, the guard was doing me no kindness. Affording me some relief, he was suggesting a final relief, was tempting me to jump. What I had taken as mercy was malice. Second: The young man below in the black cap who beckons is a collaborationist, a prisoner like the rest of us, trying to save his own life by leading us to death. And it won't work: in the end they will kill him too. Third: Although I now have the strength to hold fast to the parapet and not jump, and so have won an extension of life, a sort of victory, this means that I will presently be subjected to even more monstrous and ingenious tortures, and that a time will come when I too can stand no more and will jump.

I flail about in bed, clutch at the sheets, cry out.

THE OLDER I get, the less I know, the darker the well of time. I have a sense of waste, of a terrible, ineluctable waste, a profligacy of waste. Everything I know, all of the accumulated strategies of life, of creation, all is being swept away.

And rendered meaningless?

I don't know. There is nothing else. All of life is a trying to make something in the face of knowing that one can make nothing that stays. As I get older, the roar of the cataract, of everything being swept away, grows louder, while the making of something becomes more and more fragile and illusory. The universe is a charnelhouse. A cataract of soul pours unendingly over the brink. We all swim upstream against the overpowering current, trying at the last moment to throw something ashore, some little thing that will remain, bear witness that we were here.

And of course some things *do* remain. Collectively they comprise the culture we inherit from the past. And if we ignore the millions of lives, each with its unique vastness of spirit spilling over the brink, that culture looks quite grand. But is of no comfort. We don't contribute to it. What we try to throw ashore falls short, is lost. *All* is lost of our flimsy and flickering lives. "We are a phantom flare of grieved desire, the ghostling and phosphoric flicker of immortal time." So Thomas Wolfe thought, and so, still, do I.

Wolfe was one of the more fortunate ones. He threw a lot ashore, and it's still with us, still alive. But of no comfort to him, I might add; he's gone. It could only have mattered to him in prospect, in attitudes of hope for the future, while he still lived.

As a matter of fact I, too, should be called fortunate; for I, too, have twisted over in the white water, in the swirling current, and lofted a bit to shore. Most of my books fall out of print, but a few seem to stay. Is that of any importance? I think not. I think it doesn't matter at all. Am I kidding myself? Can I imagine a thought experiment that might test this out? Well . . . perhaps.

Suppose the consciousness that is I, that now thinks these thoughts, to be a ghost, my corporeal life having been lived say in the sixteenth century. Would it now matter to this ghost whether that actual life of four hundred years ago had been grand or nameless? Would I care whether I could, or could not, now, as a ghost, go to an encyclopedia and with my invisible hands look myself up? Hm . . . I'm not sure. I would like to know that my life had been colorful, adventurous, gallant, rather than drab, but beyond that I don't think I would care. I'm a writer; would I want to have been a famous writer? Fame I would have wanted *then*; I wouldn't *now* care. It wouldn't matter. Looking back over the now immutable past, I'd just as soon have been John Skelton as William Shakespeare. For who besides this forlorn ghost could know? And why should that ghost now care? Why even should he think back? Why, indeed, since he does not and cannot exist?

VALUE IS CERTAIN in sex and play. Of nothing else can one be sure. Laughter, dancing, sensuality—*this* is life. Guilt, anxiety, depression—*this* is death. When children race through the house laughing and screaming, chasing each other, grabbing, tearing each other's clothes, tickling and groping, jumping on sofas, throwing pillows, overturning chairs, ignoring authority, defying rules, violating boundaries, we recognize that this is life being fully lived moment by moment, that death has no part in this scene, does not exist, that this is life in its purest form, the most enviable state of being. We recognize it, but we are afraid of it, so what we experience usually is a furious disapproval, not recognizing our envy.

For we adults have become adults by virtue of designating, at the prompting of anxiety and insecurity, the more exuberant aspects of sex and play as evil, of formulating rules that forbid them, of becoming ourselves the rulekeepers and rule enforcers and infraction punishers, of spending our lives in redemptive efforts, in guilt and penance, trying to cleanse ourselves, to renounce our sin, and so achieving a measure of order, thereby gaining—what?—a clear view of the final emptiness.

THE LITTLE GIRL dancing. Natural unlearned grace. A concentrated essence of sexiness informing every movement, and every movement in perfect control. Here is the whole of meaning, of everything. This is all there is in life and when it is lost—and it is always lost!—one must keep looking.

Don't give up. Keep going as long as you can. Let that life that is anyway streaming away stream *through* you.

DIRTY OLD MEN are dirty because they are hanging on to life. Sex is the life force, and the nearer they come to death, the more urgent their desire. Thus it comes about that the drive becomes most insistent at the time when the ability to gratify it is disappearing. So they augment a waning potency by reaching down into the dirt, adding lust and aggression to hold aloft an impulse that once soared effortlessly on wings of love alone.

A FAINT BUT terrible screaming pervades the world. In the plaza at the foot of Market Street, in the humid sunshine of Sunday afternoon, near the angular opulence of the Hyatt-Regency, craftsmen with their wares: potters, jewelers, sculptors, weavers, leatherworkers, photographers, artists; their works spread out so carefully on pads, or soiled sheets, or patches of black velour; no one buying; each little display a tiny universe, so easily kicked over or blown away or bundled up and put away in the trunk of a beaten-up old car in which the young man or woman will then sit and eat a stale cheese sandwich and drink a beer.

And later, at home, I too, in my tiny universe: looking in the storeroom, in the dungeon, knowing I will never, ever, be able to clean out this place, throw away what is of no use, it's too much, too heavy, someone else will have to do it, after I've gone, someone not so attached.

It fills all the space, blows over our faces, blows from the furthermost reaches of history, a fingernail scraping an endless blackboard.

I FEEL UNEASE. A vague disturbance, distraction. Something that might get worse, might become agitation. Something important I should be doing. It is Sunday. I am free. But am not free, not at ease, cannot enjoy the world. The feeling is not in my head exactly, or my heart, but somewhere near the middle. Deep inside. Well, perhaps the heart. A vague ache, a warning: something to be done. Before I die.

A postcard from Sulka. An advertisement. I sit at my desk, look at the picture with a mournful longing that slowly becomes a pain, then drop the card in the wastebasket. Then retrieve it. The worm of envy gnaws deeper. A bed, a man lying on his side, shoulder raised, supporting himself on his left elbow, looking into the face of the young woman beside him. He is wearing a paisley silk dressing gown (that's what Sulka is trying to sell); she is in a nightgown, one breast partially exposed. Everything misty and poetic. His right arm lies across her chest. But he, *he*, if he wants, whenever he wants, she won't resist, she loves him, will permit him anything—*he* can reach under her nightgown, slowly come up her thigh, into her pubic hair, into her crotch.

That's when I feel the pain. He is very young, and very handsome. She is beautiful. Both have thick dark hair. Her pubic hair—I *know* it—is black, dense, a dark wood. A mournful panic sweeps over me. This way lies madness.

SILENTLY, IRRESISTIBLY, WE are moved backward. The crowd before us swells, stretches far ahead. The generation behind us falls away. We are backed up to the edge.

EARLY IN THE morning I arrive at my immaculate airy office, open the French doors, sink into my chair, pick up my writing of yesterday . . . put it aside, watch the wind billow the lace curtains. Misery fills my soul, much as the cool gray light wells up and fills the room. It is inadmissible. If I speak of it to my wife, she protests, reminds me how fortunate I am, of the many who live in want, in danger, in bondage. All true. And every such consideration increases my shame. If I persist, she becomes resentful, says I am dragging her down. And she's right. Such disaffection, in the midst of ease, of affluence, is

disloyalty to life. There is something disgusting about it, a fouling of the pool of life in which all are immersed.

I could perhaps deny it, but cannot give it up. It is what I am.
Inalienable. I think of the day ahead, the patients I will see,
their special varieties of trouble, of uncertainty, of suffering.
With them I have a quite special obligation to embody the possibility of arriving at an adjustment that permits the affirmation
of life. The adjustments I do in fact help them achieve—usually with more denial than is possible for me—provide them with
more basis for such affirmation than I can find within myself.

So here I am, an incontinent man, swimming around with
loved ones, friends, patients, in the pool of life, treading water,
paddling about, chatting, laughing, commenting on the weather like everybody else. If I tell them I am fouling the water, I
spoil the fun for everyone. If I keep quiet and pretend all is
well, I am in bad faith.

WE ANALYSTS ARE very defensive about our theory. As well we
might be. Conjectural excess has always been our method. "It
may be surmised that . . . " "We may assume that . . . " "It
seems possible that . . . " These phrases thread their way
through our literature, in and out, modest little bridges
between clinical finding and some new proposition designed
to explain that finding, the proposition always advanced as a
"hypothesis," thereby claiming scientific status, yet always
nonverifiable and nonfalsifiable. It comes about finally that
simply the showing of clinical data as *consonant* with a hypothesis is taken as proof of the hypothesis.

As conjectures acquire credibility by such use, and become
venerable also with age, with mere survival, insidiously they
cease to be hypotheses and come to be facts—upon which new
conjectures may then be built. And every one of us wants to do
a little building. We get out our little hammers—master
builders every one of us!—and tack on some new bit of gin-

gerbread to an already overloaded, already dangerously over-hanging, already too baroque, balcony. Our theory is now a Winchester House, that mystery house of a thousand rooms, secret doors and passageways, different levels, always chang-ing, crazy angles, one room connecting obscurely with the next, the whole thing the product of its owner's belief (Winchester's widow, I think) that so long as the house was unfinished, she would not die—*that* hypothesis having been advanced by her palmist. That's what our theory is like, and it's quite understandable we might be defensive about it.

But there's something else we assume, more basic, more important, about which we're not defensive at all. Indeed, we seem unaware of it, take it so for granted, like the air we breathe, so self-evidently true that its truth need no longer be remarked. That assumption is simply that it is possible for a human being to be well adjusted, to have a good life, that how-ever rare it may be in fact, it is in principle possible. There are a few psychoanalytic asides, always jocose, which stand as dis-claimers. "Analysis enables you to cope with the misery of real life," or "to adjust to the poverty in which it leaves you." But this is window-dressing, a specious cynicism to ward off the embarrassment of a real utopianism.

The assumption is basic and ubiquitous. Without it, we'd have to pack up our couch and ottoman and fade away. Our so-called science is married to a genuine faith: That serious and sustained misery is not inherent to human life, that it is imposed by neurotic conflict or by reality hardship; that, there-fore, if neurotic conflict is analyzed and resolved, and if reality hardship is absent, one will love and will work, will live out one's span with contentment, with real gratifications, and when the end comes will pronounce it all to have been worth while.

Of course, we say, there is always reality hardship, and that's true. But no, not *always*. For it's also true—rather blatantly, even embarrassingly, true—that many of us in America, most particularly those of us who can afford psychoanalysis, are often free of reality hardship, are in good health, have money, are well married, have suffered no loss. Are we well adjusted? Are analysts well adjusted? As a group, we are spectacularly free of reality hardship, and are very well analyzed. What would I say of my own life? Of the lives of my colleagues?

We are deceived and we have deceived others. The good life is possible when awareness is limited, but it is not possible for us. We know too much. Were we to know only the world, we'd be all right. But knowledge spills over. We know also ourselves, our fear, our destructiveness, our hunger for immortality, our oncoming death. Our knowledge subverts adjustment at the root. The misery inheres in what we are. The ideal is incoherent.

IN THE AFTERNOONS I see patients, in the mornings I write. Helping others is ephemeral; writing is my real work. Or so I have thought. But more and more I merely sit in my office in the mornings watching the lace curtains billow in and out, hearing the traffic sounds from Jackson Street, staring at the wall. I have become aware that I have been straining to write in stone. My disaffection is not that I have failed—I have the energy and the will to go on—but that the goal is illusory. Nothing can be falsified in psychoanalysis. Kohut cannot displace Hartmann. Freud wanted to be not only right, but right in such a way as would prove others wrong. In this he fails. We all fail. Freud makes his appeal—and a very powerful appeal it is—not by being preemptively right about anything, but by offering a vision of human life that makes sense of our experience. But it doesn't make complete sense, nor exclusive sense. No one is drummed out, no view is exorcised. Jung makes his appeal in the same way. And Rank and Sullivan and Horney and all the rest. A chorus of contending voices, each with a catchy tune, and each claiming to be the one true theme. How we are to make sense of our lives is not something that some great genius can get straight once and for all, but an ongoing task of interpretation in a changing field.

Earlier in my life I chafed at clinical work, would have preferred to be a full-time writer. As I have grown older, however, and have become aware of how shabby, tattered, and unread are most of those messages nailed against the wall of eternity, I have begun to feel fortunate in my work with patients, honored at being trusted with secrets that entail so much vulnerability, grateful at being able to help.

The bad thing about being old is knowing so much, which makes it impossible to learn anything new. The too-experienced eye cannot see the world afresh, has seen too much already, knows there's nothing new, sees only what it already knows to be there. So one is left behind with his wisdom; the static vision becomes stale while, unnoticed, the world turns, becomes something new.

Oh to be young again, awash in inexperience, everything to be encountered, grasped, understood, for the first time! How reclaim that seminal ignorance? How give up being the old pro?

I HAVE DEFINED and clarified the nihilistic position until it includes everything, and goodness itself becomes a random throw. Yet even so, it is unthinkable not to try. Standing by the freeway and seeing there before me in the fast lane an injured child, would I not try?

But there *is* an injured child. In Vietnam, Biafra, Bangladesh, Babi Yar—the list is endless. Always there is an injured child. Of what trying, then, am I capable, I who for so long have burrowed within, ever more deeply down and inward, who live now in an airless world of phantoms, who no longer know even where the fast lane is?

The lamentation disappears in thin air. Life offers no task with transcendent authorization, no goal the accomplishment of which can be guaranteed to have lasting value. I must accept that whatever I undertake is as risky, of both achievement and value, as darting out on that freeway. Probably I shall be killed before reaching the child, or, if I succeed in snatching him up, he will die of injuries already received—or survive to become a murderer. There's nothing sure to go on—only that it's unthinkable not to try, that there isn't anything else. If ultimate tasks are illusory one must have at the tasks near at hand, at the transient tasks, the cries for help in a confused and changing field.

I fall at times into such a brave, constructive mood. It doesn't last. The possibility of doing useful work commands no energies of mine. What these energies will respond to, and to nothing else, is a task that is faithful to the crushing and exceptionless nihilism by which I am riven and yet shot through— like Mahler's Ninth Symphony—with a vision of lyric beauty. The former without the latter is intolerable; the latter without the former is trivial. I must maintain the search for a task that will embody both. Were I to find it, energies would become available, would bend to this vision.

LIKE THE GRAY light that seeps through the lace curtains, rises as in a pool, and fills the room with muffled stillness, so longing, pain, and desire spill forth, accumulate, rise, wash over me, mount, fill the room, while I sit here alone in the still depths, feeling my way, in the dark, like a blinded ship at the bottom of a sea of fog.

STOCKBRIDGE. WHEN MY last patient leaves, I am through and could go home, but lie on the couch, cold, feeling still the warmth of another body, drawing it in. I look out at the sky. The snow has stopped, it is cold and getting colder. A rising wind has cleared the sky, and the leafless tops of elms are touched with thin winter sunshine. I get up finally and go through the routine of leaving: putting on hat and gloves, warm and dry from a day in the steam-heated building; stuffing trouser bottoms into high galoshes; snapping off the light; checking the mailbox in the deserted secretarial office; then down the hall past the popping radiator to the front door and out into the cold.

Main Street is deserted. A few houses have wreaths on the doors, colored lights in the windows. Inside, dinners are being prepared, fires are burning, dogs bark, children play. Outside is the wind. In the hospital, patients are sitting in the lounge, idling at jigsaw puzzles, reading magazines, waiting for the dinner chime. The office building behind me is empty. Everyone has gone home.

The interlacing elm branches brush together in the wind with a dry clicking sound. As I put my hand on the door handle of my car, I hear a whispering of clawed feet. High above the street a troop of squirrels, perhaps fifteen or twenty, are scampering through the smallest branches against the pale green sky. They move together, very fast, almost flying, the branches dipping to their weight and swaying in the wind— waves of soft fur fleeing from high branch to high branch, from tree to tree, in a convulsive sinuous writhing. A frantic search for food, I think, a last hopeless expedition for nuts before being caught and held in the vise of winter.

I stand there watching until they disappear, my hand on the door handle, the cold seeping through my glove. All is known. What I have done before I may do again. Spring will follow winter. What lies ahead is already past.

I AM CROUCHING in a low space. The light is dim. The far reaches of this vast room are in darkness. Forty years we have lived in this house and all around me are the pushed-aside but not yet discarded accumulations of our past. A bookcase of cleaning supplies, coffee filters, paper towels; a heap of luggage, duffel bags, overnight cases; a Danish chair of leather and gray tweed, one leg loose; Joan's loom from the sixth grade—the bit of fabric on the warp, frozen by the passing of childhood, has not grown in thirty years. A case of whiskey, wooden shutters, tables, bedsprings, toys, books, manuscripts, boxes of old checks, business records, office supplies, rugs with crumbling rubber pads. Gear belonging to Joan's former boyfriends, now scattered and replaced: scuba equipment, fins, goggles, a projection machine, a power saw. Slides, photographs, puppets, Christmas ornaments, dolls. The light is dim because these things are piled so high they block the light from the two bulbs.

From concrete floor to rough plaster ceiling is five feet; I walk deeply bent over. My back hurts. The house towers above me. My life presses down on me, bends me forward and down like a bow.

I can never sort through all this junk. Should call someone to get it, cart it all away. Don't look. Just let it go. Start over, with an empty room. At my age? I spot a box which, I remember, contains three chess sets, two of ivory, one of alabaster. Valuable things here. In a pile of rugs, I recognize the fringe of an antique Isfahan that lay on the floor of my office for twenty years. The funeral-urn design, blues and greens and violets, reds and rusts, and beside each urn the phoenix. Life springs from ashes, it's true, but new life; the old life does not spring, does not return. My life is bound to this place, to this body, to memories that will go with me as unavoidably as fillings in my teeth.

Footsteps above. Light, quick. Footsteps of utter femaleness.

The far wall of this dim space—I can just make it out—is curved. I see the impressions of the wood frame in which the concrete was poured a hundred years ago. Directly above me is the dining room. Circular. White fabric walls with elaborate delicate moldings, three pairs of high French doors opening onto a garden. Azaleas, wisteria, bougainvillaea, camellias, rhododendrons. Above each set of doors a half circle of glass, mullions radiating as in a spread fan.

High ceiling. In that room, we sit to eat together. For all these years. On the day we bought this house, forty years ago, she brought a bottle of champagne. We sat on the floor of that room and drank to each other, to the future. I still can smell the dust, the paint. How I loved it! The quality of light, the emptiness around us that was to fill up with our lives.

Directly above the dining room is our bedroom. Again the curved wall, casement windows opening over a park. Cypress, pine, blue spruce, purple plum. At night we lie on the large bed, windows open, curtains stirring slightly in the warm breeze, dim reflected light, moving leaves and branches on the white ceiling. Bodies press together, strain for oneness, achieve it for a moment, fuse, hold it, fall reluctantly, exhaustedly, back into separateness.

Above the bedroom, accessible only by a vertical ladder affixed to the wall of a closet—a closet so stuffed with old clothes, boxes, vacuum cleaners, suitcases that merely to open the door is to risk being knocked down, accessible therefore only to me—above the bedroom is the roof, the summit. The world, glittering with sun and color, opens up, lies at one's feet: bay, bridge, the Presidio, ocean liners, the Transamerica pyramid, the towering monoliths of downtown San Francisco.

This house, this living, breathing organism—holding all the markings and detritus of our lives, holding her of those quick steps and holding me, and all our past—towers up vertically over me. I am in its nethermost depths.

We call this place "the dungeon" to distinguish it from the storeroom that adjoins it, which has a seven-foot ceiling. "Where did you put it?" my wife will ask. "In the storeroom?" "No, the storeroom is full; I put it in the dungeon." "I'll never be able to find it," she will say. And indeed, she will not. Nor, probably, will I. Since the dungeon is so difficult to enter and so hard to move about in, she seldom comes here. The things stored here are heavy, and it is I who bring them.

Once here, they seldom leave. I lose track of what is here and where.

The disorder of this place does not reflect me; I am known to be exceedingly neat. This requires explanation. I am like one of those stars that undergo erratic motion explicable only by the supposition that they are twinned with nonvisible stars the masses of which account for the observed perturbations. This mess around me is my perturbation. It is she of those footsteps with whom I am twinned who leads me to behave uncharacteristically.

For she trusts things, believes that beautiful things cannot but enrich our lives, while I distrust things, know that, beautiful or not, they bring disorder, entropy, and death. So it has come about over the years that she would bring things into this house and I would throw things out. She would bring fabrics, furniture, pictures, wall hangings, musical instruments, books, phonograph records, photographs, china, vases, linens, lamps, cooking utensils, gadgets, games. And soon the blessed emptiness of our new house was lost. To preserve order, I would give things away, constantly, and the basement stayed neat. But eventually I realized that this task was endless, that I could never rest, that she would bring in new things quite as fast as I could get rid of old things, that I was doomed, therefore, to stand forever in the cellar of our lives with a shovel, trying to keep up with the avalanche coming down from above.

A time came when I rebelled. I would shovel no more. Let the stuff accumulate. Maybe eventually the backup, the back pressure, would neutralize her acquisitiveness—as the production of new automobiles might someday conceivably be halted at the factory by virtue of the highway to the city becoming so clogged with cars that there was no place for new cars to go, no room for them even to roll off the assembly line.

"Isn't that the most wonderful chair?" she says; we are in a store of Scandinavian furniture. "Look at the curve of the arms. Like the wings of a bird. It would be just perfect in our living room—where the blue chair is now. That blue chair is getting shabby anyway. We should replace it." "Where will we put it?" I ask. "Maybe in Joan's room." "There's no space left in Joan's room." "Well . . . the dungeon then." "There's no space left in the dungeon," I tell her. "Well, we'll just have to give some things away . . . to make some space."

"Very well," I say in my vast and patient deviousness, "but let's don't buy this new chair until we have first done that giving away of some things in the dungeon so there will be a place to put the blue chair, so that this new bird chair can go in the living room."

Sadly, she acquiesces; we pass on through the store. And once home, of course, she forgets about looking in the dungeon, has no time and no interest for sorting through and disposing of this mess.

I WALK ABOUT the house, can't sit still. It feels like home yet not like home. It's too still, too quiet. I look out on the smeared roofs of the houses below and want something to happen, want to go somewhere. I'm like my grandfather in his last days.

As a young man, my grandfather built his big house in Marion, Louisiana. Lived there with my grandmother for fifty years. In the same house. He was eighty-three when she died, then went downhill fast. Became silent, restless, would wander about the house, looking for something, he didn't know what, would get dressed as if he were going somewhere. Black suit, white shirt, black string tie, cane, hat. Would sit on the front porch in the swing, waiting, looking for something. Talked to himself, nobody could understand what he was saying.

He would seek me out, tug on my arm. "I'm ready now, son, I want to go home." "You *are* home, Grandpa," I would tell him; "this *is* home." I'd take him into his room, show him his clothes, his pipes, his bed. He would nod absently, would go back out on the front porch, sit in the swing, resume his waiting. And after a while he'd be back, tapping on my shoulder, a restless shuffle in his high, laced black shoes, a feverish alienation in his eyes. "I want to go home now, son." "All right, Grandpa, I'll take you home."

He'd put on his hat and I'd take him by the arm, help him down the steps, out the front walk, through the gate, would hoist him up into the old Chevy. Then I'd drive around town . . . would stop at Spence Allen's place. "Is that home, Grandpa?" He would shake his head and we'd go on. I'd stop at Grover Hopkins's place. "Is this home, Grandpa?" He'd look it over carefully and shake his head.

I'd keep driving around, slowly, to all the places he knew. And he would keep looking. "When you see a place that looks like home, Grandpa, just say the word and I'll stop and let you out." And he would nod and brush his fingers against his lips, always quivering a bit, and would keep looking while I drove around the parish.

Sometimes he would discover in some faint overgrown path into the woods a promise of the haven he sought. "Try down there, son." And I'd turn in until stopped by underbrush and fallen trees. And of course he wouldn't find it, and finally I'd drive back home. "Is this it, Grandpa?" "I guess so, son," he would say, beginning to climb down, disappointment in his voice. And I'd take him into the house and for a while he'd be content. But not for long. The next day he would get his cane and his hat and be tugging at my arm again. "I want to go home, son."

FIVE YEARS OLD, too young for school. Skinny arms and legs sticking out from skimpy pants and short-sleeve shirt. When the older boys got back from school, I went to Jimmy's house to play. Five boys had arranged themselves in a circle, were throwing a ball one to another in sequence. I put myself in the circle, but when my turn came, the ball sailed over my head to the next in line. An oversight, perhaps; I waited for the next round. When passed over again, I complained. They did not seem to hear.

My complaint grew louder, became pleading. Again and again the ball flew over my head. I jumped but could not reach it, wailed, went to my friend who usually was willing to play with me, tugged on his sleeve, "Let me play, Jimmy! Throw it to me too! Please, Jimmy!" Jimmy shrugged, threw the ball over my head. I began to cry. "It's not fair!"

I was enraged, wanted to retaliate, to walk away. But could not reject them so long as they would not see me, would not hear. And because they were denying my existence, I could not give up trying to enter their circle. I began to run after the ball, tried to intercept throws, but when I managed to position myself before the next receiver, the order would change, the ball going instead to someone else. I ran back and forth, in and out, never finding a way to become a part. It was a magic circle, it joined them, excluded me. I was a nonperson.

Eventually I gave up, sat down at some distance, exhausted, disheartened, watched the ball fly around, one to another, in sequences of infinite desirability. It was too painful to watch, I lowered my head, scratched in the dirt. When my crying stopped, the boys, tired of the game, stood about idly, bored, wondered what to do next. "Here, Allen," Jimmy said, as if to a dog, and tossed me the now unwanted ball. The boys huddled, came to a decision, set off together. "Where are we going?" I asked, following after. But again could not make myself heard. I ran to keep up, but they ran faster, and came presently to a thicket which with their long pants they could push through, whereas I, with bare legs, was turned back bleeding. The boys disappeared, their laughter grew fainter, died away. I extricated myself from the brush, walked back toward Jimmy's house. It was getting dark. There was a strong and cold wind. I was whimpering. Maybe crying.

Then there was my mother standing before me in her long

brown coat. "A norther has come up," she said, taking my hand. "All of a sudden. That's why it's so dark and cold." I looked up. Black clouds were rushing across the sky. She wiped my nose. "We must go home." The pebbles hurt my bare feet; I hopped and lurched, holding her hand, trying to avoid the sharper stones. My teeth were chattering, the skin of my arms and legs became goose flesh.

My mother stopped, opened her coat. "Come inside," she said. She folded me into the coat, buttoned it in front of me. We proceeded awkwardly, my shoulder against her thigh, my head alongside her hip, enveloped in darkness, in warmth, in the smell of her body. She was wearing an apron, and there was a smell also of food—onions and something fried. She must have been cooking supper when the norther hit. And stopped to come get me.

It was difficult to walk; we went slowly. I couldn't see anything ahead, but looking down could see the ground where I was putting my feet. I was getting warm in that germinal darkness. My teeth stopped chattering, my knees stopped shaking. I was aware of the powerful movement of her hip against my cheek, the sense of a large bone moving under strong muscles. Aware also that it was difficult for her to walk with me buttoned in. Occasionally she stumbled. And just then, for the first time, I became aware of goodness. Of goodness as a special quality, like evil, which a person may or may not possess. She doesn't *have* to do this, I thought. It's not necessary. I'm cold, but I could make it home all right.

What she gave me could not have been demanded, I would never have thought to ask. All afternoon I had been demanding something to which it seemed I had a right, and had been denied; yet here was a good to which I had no right, freely offered. No trade. Nothing asked in return.

THE MEANING OF life is in that coat: it is the home to which one belonged as a child. If you're lucky, you never lose it; it simply evolves, smoothly and continuously, into that larger, more abstract home of religion, or perhaps, in a secular vein, into clan or community or ideology. Meaninglessness means homelessness. When home is lost and the nightmares begin, that's when one goes in quest of meaning.

And one has the impression then of reaching outward and forward, of delving into something *out there*, of grappling with the world, trying to penetrate a mystery; and it seems that one has only just come to recognize the existence of this most fundamental problem, a problem that has been there all along, but that only now, just possibly, has one arrived at the capacity to solve, or at least to try. But this is retrospective falsification. The problem has not been there all along; it came into being only with the loss of home, and the attempt to solve it is not an effort to create something new but to recreate something old. It is a quest backward. One is trying to refashion, in a form acceptable to an intellectualizing adult, the home of one's childhood.

How to live? Who knows the question knows not how. Who knows not the question cannot tell.

In those days, everything seemed different. It seemed possible to organize one's life, to resist the tide of entropy, to impose form. In some fundamental sense, life seemed understandable if one went at it with enough will and intelligence. Now everything seems different. Life is not to be managed—or shaped or directed, it is not even to be understood. Life is to be lost. And the only question is whether with grievance or with generosity and grace.

JOAN THROWS A ball for Monty. Out of the trees, suddenly, comes a large yellow dog, attacks, is tearing at her dog. She weeps desperately. The violence and the tears are everywhere—behind a tree, beneath a leaf, in the smiles of a summer day. Escape, forget for a while, but not for long.

I separate the dogs and her sobs diminish, but one day it will be me, or someone else dear to her, and she'll be sobbing again in just such helplessness. Our safe world may be lost in the spite, the vanity, the self-indulgent fit of any one of our tyrants, and the sobbing children of Vietnam, the screaming mothers, will be all around us. The crazy violence that is everywhere, promiscuous, flares up in an instant, with no more warning, no more meaning, no more reason than a dogfight. How little time for laughter, how brief our innocence of what lies in wait.

What can I do with what I know? What is my task?

Canetti: "Oh priest of signs, disquieted creature, caught in the temple of all alphabets, your life will soon be over. What have you seen? What have you feared? What have you accomplished?"

MY WIFE HAS built for me a new study. Blue ceiling, birch walls, wonderful smell of new lumber. I feel a deepening intolerance of apathy, of not making anything, of sliding downhill on an old life that is really over.

He who has a message, who deals in salvation, writes a book of structured argument, of hierarchic order, of reasons in sequence. Not I. My life is all searching, never finding. I bear witness to what I have seen—a maze of roads, conflicting signs, freeways that end on nowhere, angelic maidens who fall under a spell and turn drab, far-reaching insights that become inert and explain nothing, blueprints of reason that twist out of shape and vanish with a twang in a minor key.

I have always been too guilty to be happy. Guilt such as mine threatens life itself. The first task, therefore—and never has there been time for a second—is to fend off an inner accusation that threatens to annihilate. This I have done, by work, day after day after day, and so life has passed, and looking back I can see I've fought my demons to a draw, or a lit-

tle better, but where, lost to me, was the music, the laughing
in the night?

BEHOLD THE MAN of reason. Regard him in his work. He has
struggled with this problem all his life. Solve it here in one
guise and it appears there in another, as if a different problem.
He is getting very old when he understands finally its true and
single nature: not knowing how to live.

Such an insight, you might think, would cast him down, but
he feels hope, exhilaration. It's better, he thinks, to have one
big problem than a bagful of small ones. You can concentrate
your efforts, create a single strategy. How, then, does one learn
how to live? One must search, see what can be seen, analyze,
make connections, relate things to each other in casual
sequences. For a rational man, there is no other way than the
way of intelligence to learn anything. But in learning how to
live, intellect is treacherous, for life is a matter of rhythms,
while intellect reduces rhythms to law.

He goes back to Hegel, to Nietzsche, to the pragmatists, the
positivists, the dialectical materialists, ransacks the old closet
of philosophy, fumbles around there in the dark as he has so
often in the past, but now with a clearer sense of what he is
looking for. He goes back to the poets, to the *Elegies* and the letters of Rilke, the effete but ruthlessly honest meditations of
Eliot; returns to the searchers after God: Pascal, Kierkegaard,
Teilhard de Chardin.

He has learned nothing, is still the student, a doomed cen-
tipede unable to correlate all those legs, falling down, getting
up, trying again, always signing up for another course: "The
Anatomy of Legs," "Legs, Their Physiology and Biochemistry,"
"Advanced Leg Dynamics," and now, still hoping, a yet more
advanced course—"How to Walk." All these courses have in
common the method of intelligence: they take the problem
apart, carefully, piece by piece, seeking hidden relationships.

.He hopes to find the rhythm by dismantling the melody, examining each beat separately.

Look at him, age sixteen, at a high school dance, already a master of this methodology. With great yearning he watches the dancers, remains aloof. Cautiously he moves along the wall, simulates nonchalance, as if at home in such gatherings. He smiles, nods, leans against a door, and, having been shown in a thousand advertisements the connection between poise and smoking, lights a cigarette. He feels dizzy, coughs, moves on, chats with a teacher, makes it appear he is taking but a brief break from the dancing.

In fact, he is watching the dancing feet. How is it done? What is the formula? He is diagramming the movement. What is the excursion of each foot? How far? In what direction? What sequence? Now he looks at the faces of the girls. How do you tell which one, on being asked, will say yes? What is the formula for that?

Suddenly before him is a girl with dark flowing hair and smiling eyes, and with every beat of the music her body registers a slight response, a resonance, which wants to become a full participation. Along his sides the trickle of sweat, the smell of fear. "Hello, Jan," he says. His mouth is paper-dry, he swallows, waves a hand casually toward the dancers. "Reminds me of that scene in *Gatsby*, the summer night, couples swaying under the paper lanterns, and that *marvelous* line, 'old men pushing young girls backward in eternal graceless circles.' " He nods, moves on; and Jan, who sailed into his life like a comet, trailing glittering promise, is swept away, lost.

MY WHOLE LIFE has been given over to this search and I have found nothing. I'm growing old and still know not how to live. It's already too late to do much with the answer, which, in any event, seems still remote.

One day, though, I shall have it. An intimation of final justice tells me this quest shall not have been in vain. Like the tourist who, avid to buy, receives his letter of credit only as he is departing the country of bargains, I shall be unable to use it, but will count it a victory in principle.

WE ARE PLUNGING down a cataract, and what's important is to call out. Not for help, there is no help. Not in despair—what can anyone do but shrug, look away? But to give a signal. A gesture of love and humor to acknowledge drowning so others who drown will know they are not alone. We are all drowning; deny it with blindness, transcend it with laughter. The laughter I seek is that which looks straight in the eye of despair and laughs. The proper subjects for comedy are fear, loneliness, and death.

Maybe there is no meaning but only life; and in art, no meaning but only the illusion of life. Maybe that's the whole thing: To observe life so closely, to search it out so carefully, with so much love, that it comes alive, that it *is*.

A HOLIDAY IN summer. I go in the afternoon in bright sunshine to sit in a dark and nearly empty theater. As I wait for the film to begin, the sour loneliness of the place settles on my spirit. Yesterday's cigarette smoke in the air, balls of hardened gum under the armrests, popcorn and candy wrappers on the floor. I and a few other bleak souls wait dumbly like oxen in the rain for deliverance, each of us isolated in the drizzle of his own everyday misery.

The house darkens, the music begins, the screen is illuminated, deliverance is at hand. *The Bicycle Thief.* The few of us sitting there, dispersed, walled off from each other by pain and distrust, by a kind of stubborn uncaring, become a community as we watch. We are shown a poor man trying to find work. We see his wife, his son, we feel their fear, the loom of hunger. Gradually de Sica's love of this man makes him come alive, makes him human. The thief who steals his bicycle is faceless, beyond notice, one of the ignominious and detestable of the earth. All our sympathy goes to his victim who, without the bicycle, will lose his job. We follow him in his desperate search, feel with him, suffer his frustration, enter his despair, finally *become* him—then *he* steals a bicycle! And suddenly *we* have stolen a bicycle, are one with all men, high and low, good and bad, and weep for all that is faceless and voiceless and moves with heavy heart over the dark earth.

What a grand thing de Sica does, what a great and disinterested love to take as its object this limited, thwarted, and weak man, and, by going out to him with such caring, such patient observing, to make him not only live—though that's miracle enough—but our brother! I most deeply salute a man with the soul to do that. And if ever I find myself seeking out the privileged, the interesting, the beautiful, I hope I will remember the bicycle thief and that I am he.

THE ONCE TOUGH, rubbery skin hangs over vanished muscles as a film, a terrifying drapery. Everything slips away: memory, vision, hearing, teeth, unable finally to tie your shoes, to hoist a suitcase to an overhead bin. Should one not be ashamed of hanging on so long?

Gogol died at forty-three; Kleist made a quick exit at thirty-four, taking his girlfriend with him. Schubert had sung his last song at thirty-one, Keats at twenty-six, Shelley at thirty, Byron ("So we'll go no more a'roving . . . ") at thirty-six, et cetera. (What am I doing? Claiming status by shared mortality?)

While I am a long time dying. When do we begin to die? And when are we done with it? Perhaps I am dead already. Would I know? When does life end? Not the last heartbeat—that doesn't matter so much—but the loss of meaning. And what is meaning?

What we are drifting toward, that dread thing, is the loss of the capacity to be loved. It happens silently; we don't notice. *They* notice, *they* know, but they don't tell us, they pretend. (Perhaps an animal might tell you: Freud knew only when the stench of his cancer was such that, though his family behaved as always, his dog would no longer come near him.) They deny, they affirm love, they declare love, but it's not love they then offer but compassion, duty, respect, sometimes fear—because we light the ugly way that they too will pass. So we never know when it happens. We die in the palsied spilling of soup, the dripping nose, the colostomy, the incontinence, we die over a cup of tea, a quiver of lip.

What is there to love when flesh has gone? Is there anything else? All noble qualities of mind may remain, but are they, without flesh, enough? Can the wasted one still love another? Is that enough?

"What do you suppose an embrace of mine would be worth now?" asks the AIDS-ravaged Harold Brodkey, recalling the myth of his sexual irresistibility.

WE LIVE BY attachment, not by reason. That's why love is primary: there is no value without caring, and caring is loving. If, looking about at the world, one finds no one and no thing to love, no bird, no tree, no flower worth caring about, the world is without value; and then, in fatal consequence, one's own life is without value.

But if, looking about at the world, one finds someone to love, or perhaps not a person but a dog, or maybe only a plant that wants water and needs sunshine, or maybe not even anything living but a thing—an old house that has sheltered us, that has creaked and moaned in the storms of winter—then one has something to live for, and in consequence, one's own life is worth preserving. That's the point: one's own life has value only because one cares for others. And one cares *without a reason!* Without reflection, without the weighing of profit and loss. The caring that justifies everything else is itself without justification. It is a leap.

Attachments grow in the dark, like roots. Silently, invisibly, they extend themselves in heart-soil, anchoring us in the world. To go on living then is not elective; we cannot depart this life, we are held by invincible tendrils.

I SMELL MY death on the wind, want to see something of beauty and nobility in the time that is left, to enlarge consciousness. I adjure myself: Stay with the main show, do not be drawn off into sideshows, diversions, entertainments. Do only what you are most solemnly charged to do. Whatever is elective is a turning away. There in the big top a man is hanging by his teeth, twisting, spinning, spotlights playing over him, the drums beginning to roll. He's going to fall and nothing can be done, no net, but in the moments remaining he may yet achieve something remarkable, a glittering gesture, a movement perhaps of breathtaking beauty.

The main show is the search. It mounts on despair, spins there above you. Any turning away to watch the dancing bears is a betrayal of the dangling man. Hold fast, stay with him, watch the twists and turns of his brief agony, study his condition. What in this fateful moment can he still do?

Is IT NOT time? Whom do I address? Time to take up again the seeking out of those faint footprints in the night, to try again, perhaps to hope again, and, beyond the trying, to seek the means to keep on seeking when nothing is found.

SOMETIMES I—EVEN I!—feel a wild and deep joyousness, the exaltation of cold wind on one's face when one is young.

IN THE DEPARTMENT store. Overcoat collar turned up, scarf over my left shoulder, black hat low over my eyes, I wait. My wife is in the ladies' room. Christmas crowds flow around me. Swirl, eddy. I stand motionless against a pillar. Minutes pass.

I turn my head, catch a woman in the moment of her jaw going slack, her lips parting. Astonishment sweeps over her face. She veers toward me, arm outstretched, beginning to smile. She has a child in tow. "Oh, my God! I didn't think you were real! Then you *moved!*" She laughs slightly, a dark, rich laugh, touches my arm. Through my jacket I feel her fingers. Again that slight laugh, relief and wonderment. Her large gray eyes make friendly contact: Though unexpected, I, refugee mannequin, am being welcomed to the realm of flesh. She nods, passes on.

Where is she? Where has she gone? I want to grab her, find her flesh under my fingers, feel it give, secure my reality in her yielding.

A FAST-MOVING TRAIN, teeming with people. A great din. All speak together, all struggle to be heard. The rocking motion throws us side to side. Rumble and clatter of wheels, groan and creak of metal. In some of the cars people are fighting, hurl each other back and forth, out the doors, out the windows. More crowded now, more difficult to move. I am pushed backward, forced to the outside, am clinging with fingertips. Cinders, the assaulting wind, the driving rain. Vision blurs, the landscape is featureless and dark. No lights, no homes, no roads. Fingers loosen. Music from within. A waltz. Ah . . . they're dancing.

I will leave this sweet monster soon. Rounding a curve, it will fling me away. Without slowing, it will hurtle on, *rackety-rackety-rackety*, *clackety-clackety-clackety*, without me, through the night.

CPSIA information can be obtained at www.ICGtesting.com
Printed in the USA
236514LV00003B/63/P